Modi
to
Moditva
An Uncensored Truth

Attention Authors

'We Convert Fighters into Writers'. That's the motto of Manas Publications since more than four decades. Our message to the world is that India can win the battle not only by the bullet but also by the pen. There is no dearth of intellectuals in our country, but their knowledge is confined to them only. No sincere effort has been made by any other publisher to channelise their knowledge in national interest. That is why the talent of a large number of intellectuals remains latent. An author transforms his knowledge into a manuscript, and it is our job to spread his/her knowledge by converting it into a beautiful book. For over four decades, Manas has been motivating the intellectuals by publishing their manuscripts and would like to publish your manuscript too. So if you or your colleagues have any manuscript ready for publication or are working on it, kindly contact us with detailed synopsis and list of contents. We will transform your work into a valuable publication. If you wish, we can also suggest you the suitable subjects for writing the books related to your area of expertise. Manas is known for its publishing quality and commitments. We take utmost care in production and give wide publicity to the book as well as its author through our national and international distribution network.

Modi
to
Moditva

An Uncensored Truth

Nirendra Dev
Senior Journalist

Manas Publications
(We Convert Fighters into Writers)
New Delhi-110002 (INDIA)

MANAS PUBLICATIONS
(We Convert Fighters into Writers)
(Publishers, Library Suppliers, Importers & Exporters)
4402/5-A, Ansari Road (Opp HDFC Bank)
Darya Ganj, New Delhi-110 002 (India)
Off. ✆ 23260783, 23265523, Fax: 011-23272766
E-mail: manaspublications@vsnl.com
manaspublications@gmail.com

ISBN 978-81-7049-446-1
₹ 595/-

Designed at
Manas Publications

Printed in India at
HS Offsets, Delhi
and published by Mrs Suman Lata for
Manas Publications, 4402/5-A,
Ansari Road (Opp HDFC Bank),
Darya Ganj, New Delhi-110 002 (INDIA)

Contents

Acknowledgements

Journalists and the journalism had fascinated me from the very beginning. One obvious reason for this is my intuition to know and study more about the unknowns. The research and writing of this book would not have been possible without my being a journalist.

The Gujarat and Narendra Modi phenomenon in my life - both the riots of 2002 and the 'development model, *Sabka Saath Sabka Vikas*' - is part of that adventure. So, I ought to be grateful to my profession for giving me the opportunity to work in and on Gujarat.

Writing on Gujarat in circa 2011-12 is truly like revisiting the state and its socio-political history in the contemporary setting. My first hand experience on Gujarat came rather in its unfortunate hours of 2002 incidents. I bow down in gratitude before all those friends, police officials, social workers and *netas* of all hues - with whom I interacted during the turbulent period.

Back in the North East, when I started as a journalist I do recall, most of my friends had found promising careers in engineering, banks, teaching and the more lucky ones into government jobs like Accountant General Office or even Meghalaya Police. Many of my contemporaries not only entertained desires for adventurism in romance, some of them were neck-deep in love and affairs. These hardly attracted me; though I must confess that like all normal youths I too had admiration for a few select good looking young ladies and yes, I continue to admire even now and have fond memories of some of them.

Therefore, I must thank those who anchored my career and life all these years. That would definitely include my parents and family members, especially my daughter Tanvi, a galaxy of journalist friends in North East, in Gujarat and of course in Delhi and Mumbai where I have served. I must make mention about the special love of my daughter and her gang of cousins – Adi, Anku, Khushie and Tirtho – that give me all the vital energy.

No gratitude in my life can be complete without mentioning about my younger brother, Nirmal Kumar Deb, fondly called Raja.

Thanks are due to my friend Supratim Sanyal of Washington Bangla Radio for patronising me with a radio interview wherein I was constantly grilled about my next offering. I am highly appreciative of the thoughtful feedback from a few keen Gujarat watchers including government officials and retired intelligence personnel who have preferred to stay unnamed.

I must also thank my colleagues in *The Statesman* and dear friend Vivek Garg of Manas Publications. The web technology and liberal references made to the media reports ought to be mentioned.

Despite the support, and encouragement from common readers for patronising my previous works, the contents and the shortcomings of this book are all mine.

PREFACE

SEARCH FOR THE SOUL

The most fascinating part of journalism, I can bet on, is that it helps you to go against the tide. As I get ready to submit the manuscript, I am aware, this book would give the impression of being pro-Modi and even 'communally and politically biased'; on the other hand there are many pages which would be dismissed as clear testimony of my inclination towards 'pseudo-secularism'. Is your book politically correct, a close friend of mine Samir Kar Purkayastha, a Guwahati-based journalist had asked me when he came to know about my venture?

My write-up often reflects diametrically opposite dimensions and so, I could be wrong.

The 2002 riots is a too strong and powerful influence in Gujarat graph that it cannot be easily erased by a decade of development model as is pursued relentlessly by the state Chief Minister Narendra Damodardas Modi, undoubtedly the principal protagonist in Gujarat polity and also in this book.

In 2002, the English media in particular in the country and also the western countries like the European Union and the US made their intention clear about their assessment regarding Gujarat, and more particularly perhaps on the people of Gujarat. My assessment was that the killings of a community could take place only on a soil 'fertile' with religious 'prejudices'.

There was truly a climax situation as hardliner communalism had assumed ominous spectre in a state, which otherwise took pride in a growth rate equalling that of China.

The real challenge in writing a book on Gujarat lies in understanding and explaining well this paradox.

Like any complex society, Gujarat poses special problems for a journalist not only while reporting a communal violence, as was in 2002, but also when one is sitting miles away and years after that plans to write a book on the state.

Unlike scientific inventions, in social science, there are hardly any drastically new and original ideas. Therefore, this book owes in more ways than one its credit to a plethora of studies, media reports, analysis by political commentators and of course the interviews I had with people including from both sides of the political divide.

This book like any social study is based on opinion of individuals and analysis by political commentators and the politicians themselves. But dealing in futuristic scenario, it is also an avalanche of maybes and ifs. The limitations are all mine, but these are not my excuses. There is a sincere inability on my part to speak with precision and certainty about the short-term and long-term future of Gujarat and its chief protagonist, Narendra Modi.

There is no claim in this book about any kind of prophecy. Rather it is a collection of sincere analyses. Gujarat is truly a proof of the statement that prosperity alone does not lead to idealism of secular values or modernisation, tolerance and accommodation.

In course of working on the book, the Human Development Report by United Nations Development Programme (UNDP) 2011 was launched. Undoubtedly, it touched upon an issue discussed several times in this book that economic growth is no criterion of human development or a happy nation state.

In Gujarat, the multi-pronged developments have come; but the social prosperity is not accompanied by human development or the moral order.

In another report, 'India Human Development Report' released by the Planning Commission and the Government of India, it was stated that despite impressive growth, Gujarat has not been able to reduce malnourishment levels, while Uttar Pradesh and Bihar, the two known most backward hubs in the country, have done better in improving the lot of their marginalised dalits and tribals.

Many say, the moral order as was understood traditionally and cherished in folktales is increasingly vanishing under the pressure of survival and challenges associated with so called modernisation and materialistic comforts. This is no doubt a national and also a global experience. But in Gujarat, the core values are perhaps vanishing faster, I say this with no intention to hurt the sentiments of the locals and with all respect for the highly enterprising skills of the people of Gujarat.

The joint families are breaking into nuclear ones sometime by design sometime by deceiving the simpleton and traditional parents. With modern education, what is expected is that legalistic moral codes would prevail. But the 2002 incidents and loot carried on by the middle class displaying the baser human instincts only proved that there was collapse of social leadership. It was a case of virtual decay of the social values. When middle class men, women and youngsters took to looting of malls, the transformation was telling. The intelligentsia has also perhaps failed to appeal to the commoners especially on issues bordering religious belief. And under Modi, it's largely alleged that there has been hardly any attempt from the state to introduce any coherent moral order.

In fact, not only Modi, the vices like saffronisation of the village home guards and state police was near complete even under Modi's illustrious predecessor Keshubhai Patel and the late Haren Pandya, whose murder is a keenly seen legal battle today. The BJP insiders say, the real reason for the cold war that existed between Pandya and Modi was this uncompromising commitment to Hindutva of the two leaders and who will really steal the limelight of the legacy. ***Moditva*** is definitely a shining feature of this very legacy one is talking about. Post-Godhra 'handling' had enhanced Modi's image as much it overshadowed the late Haren Pandya, who was also Minister of State for Home under Keshubhai Patel.

And once VHP and other Sangh Parivar elements got the upper hand, the voice of tolerance, accommodation and respect for other religious believers vanished. "The intelligentsia were either threatened or suppressed" and only the likes of Pravin Togadia were at liberty to propagate their viewpoints.

Like developments everywhere, in Gujarat too, the 'development model' of Modi has its share of gainers and losers. For obvious reasons, the Modi detractors are pinning down on the losses and negativity. Losers are generally from lower strata of the society – the landless and displaced. The affected belonged to poorer background economically and backward castes got marginalised and isolated in some pockets. On the contrary, the gainers are from upper echelons of the society – Patidars and those with certain assets and skill and education to capitalise on. We take a close look at these issues too.

Another impact of socio-development change is always that the social institutions get compartmentalised and fractionated giving way to certain contradictions in social practices. People in Gujarat tend to be modern, prefer pizzas as regular snacks but would opt for 'Jain Pizzas' and hate 'meat eaters'. Incidentally, the refrain in Ahmedabad is that the world's first 'vege-all' Pizza Hut came in Ahmedabad only.

The loss of community also means reinforcing tendencies towards factionalism along with complete collapse of collective responsibility and welfare. More the modern day's development, each man becomes an island of his self creation.

These compartmentalised living also result in 'ghettoization' of cities. Like Mumbai, a city with overwhelming Gujaratis, major Gujarat cities like Ahmedabad and Baroda are gradually getting ghettoized with 'mini Pakistan' name given to Muslim-dominated old city area very conveniently.

The good old saying, the glass is half-full or half-empty applies to all dynamic human conditions. The beauty of the thing lies in the beholder's eyes. This book suggests that there is a need to come to judgements on issues and events. There are both positive aspects and the negativity of any situation. Analysts often point to one or the other aspect and draw their conclusions. There are those who see positive flashpoints in a situation and consider them as adequate justification for lauding what happened. Narendra Modi and his admirers in and outside BJP are exactly doing the same. At the same time, there are others, who cannot wash off the gory memories of 2002.

I belong to neither side; though the anti-Muslim riots is something I disapprove of with all my sincerity as I firmly believe if Godhra train inferno was wrong the riots too were equally unjustified. Two wrongs do not make it right. Therefore, this book tries to show how the positives and the negatives can come together to help reach a judgement about the net effect, though it is not necessarily a balanced prodigy.

Even by 2001, around the time Modi replaced Keshubhai Patel, Gujarat was one of the four top developing states of India. A Planning Commission report had then observed that "the enterprising population of Gujarat supported by its progressive leadership" had brought the state in the forefront of economic development. The state economy had always grown at a 'faster rate' than the national economy much before Modi or today's hyped Moditva had come in the forefront. The secondary and tertiary sectors in the state had shown a consistent higher growth rate as compared to all India figures and the state had highly diversified sources of income.

BJP and Narendra Modi, therefore, would do well to keep in mind that they should not underestimate the voters' intellect. Any attempt especially to monopolise information or bank singularly on own trumpet or propaganda has boomeranged on every such regimes. Lately, this has happened in the left-citadel West Bengal. The Communists globally have got the feel of it after Soviet Union. Closer home in India, the Congress party experienced it after emergency and also aftermath of Bofors scam controversy. The Congress thought Bofors will be like any other issue, but the party with 400 plus strength in the Lok Sabha was ousted and more so the family of Nehru-Indira legacy from 7 Race Cource Road, the official Prime Minister's residence for over 20 years. So did BJP. The saffron party strategists and their Sangh Parivar sympathisers thought Gujarat riots will be a bygone case under the hyped campaign of 'India Shining'. They lost power in 2004.

Finally, one must say, this book would fail those who want to know, what really sparked off the inferno at Godhra railway station on February 27, 2002 or how Modi rebuked some ministers in his cabin in front of babus. This book will not tell either whether Modi will come out unscathed in the series of trials of cases related to the Gujarat riots or that he would end up facing chargesheet.

Like most journalistic works, this book is not a scholarly historical perspective either on Moditva, his development or the politics of communalism. Journalism is fondly also described as a literature in hurry. This book is only an attempt to look at the history as it unravels. It is also recording of an episode in contemporary history in hurry. It is a mixture of pure reportage, journalistic analysis and accumulation of my first hand knowledge and experience out of works in Gujarat and about Gujarat. I have also resisted the temptation to delve deeply into the past or into the day-to-day happening in the government.

There are other issues in developments. Agriculture, ideally as well as culturally for India, is the best means of man's livelihood. But that ideological statement has fallen flat in today's Gujarat, wherein the Chief Minister is in a tiring hurry to enhance his 'image' by pushing industries and facilitating easy and smooth grazing for industries especially the large houses, both from within the country and abroad. Moreover, along with the rest of India, Gujarat too needs to take a closer look at issues as strongly argued by the Union Agriculture Minister, Sharad Pawar that the successful implementation of UPA's flagship scheme MGNREGA has enhanced the purchasing power of rural labour class too and taken them off the fields. Sociologists believe that if education spreads unemployment and dependency, it is far dangerous than ignorance and illiteracy.

On the political debate, we discuss whether Modi is in direct conflict with his long-time mentor LK Advani; Modi himself on 7th November, 2011, sought to clarify that all is well between the two.

But in May 2012 as Modi and BJP President stuck a deal, the veteran Advani, BJP's original mascot stayed away from party's Mumbai rally and also flayed the leadership for inept handling of situations.

On May 31, 2012, the day BJP and other opposition parties staged *Bharat Bandh* against petrol price hike; in his blog, Advani wrote: "The mood within the party these days is not upbeat. The results in Uttar Pradesh, the manner in which the party welcomed BSP ministers who were removed by Mayawati on charges of corruption, the party's handling of Jharkhand and Karnataka – all these events have undermined the party's campaign against corruption".

He further wrote: "I had said at the Core Group meeting that if people are today angry with the UPA government, they are also disappointed with us. The situation, I said, calls for introspection".

We will try to understand the facets more intimately.

Gujarat has attained a reputation for hustle-bustle. True, this reputation is largely deserved, but at times undeserved too. The Godhra and post-Godhra incidents have eliminated logic and ethics as social and political factors for the state. In the end, one must say, Gujarat's problems are enormous and any attempt to sum them up will be fragmented, patchy and thus appear erratic and also superficial. This book will be no exception, I am afraid.

Introduction

History is rightly described as the most accommodating affair. Its pages are full of mortal men and women anointed with immortality. It's a different matter that these spaces are not always given as honour or accolades. My profession, journalism, describes these characters better – 'newsmakers'. Since 2002 February, when the ill-fated S-6 compartment of Sabarmati Express was burnt in Godhra and the subsequent incidents in the state of Gujarat, the Chief Minister Narendra Damodardas Modi has easily attained for himself the crown of 'newsmaker' for reasons more than one – year after year.

Therefore, the book at hand deals with many aspects on expected lines – on the politics of country's foremost headline hunter; and some, of course, would provoke disagreements and intense debate. From the very beginning when I discussed about the project with a few select professional friends, I have been cautioned that the project sounds too ambitious and at the same time bound to be 'misunderstood' by several quarters.

As the book was near completion and I tried to take a relook at the first few pages, I found on one side, the book would give the impression of being pro-Modi and even 'communally and politically biased'. On the other hand, there are many pages which would be dismissed as an inclination towards pseudo-secularism. But I should not be blamed for these diametrically opposite dimensions.

One likes it or not, the 2002 riots have left a permanent scar mark about Gujarat. Everybody is busy sharing his or her assessment about Gujarat, and more particularly perhaps on the people of Gujarat in the wake of the post-Godhra riots and the two successful Assembly elections bagged by BJP under Modi's leadership.

In 2005, the US denied visa to Modi. But in 2011, that means - over nine and half years after the incidents, a report drawn up by the US Congressional Research Service (CRS) identified Gujarat under the same Narendra Modi as offering perhaps the best example of 'effective governance' and impressive development in India. The author is aware that this is not the official US administration assessment; but the report had definitely fetched Modi some 'good publicity' braving against perhaps daily bombardment of criticism of his functioning. It's altogether a different matter that within days in a different report, the US administration's notion about Modi and the state of Gujarat was reported in a different language.

"To place the development in context, it must be known that CRS reports are scholarly analyses of an issue or set of issues. These reports are not intended to serve as a position that the US Congress has taken or may be taking", wrote my good friend and a senior colleague KV Prasad in his report for *The Hindu* on September 15, 2011. Two days after the US Congressional report made news, Prasad argued eloquently that the document was essentially a research paper and not a Congressional assessment per se.

"While it may suit political parties to amplify observations made in the report for the consumption of the domestic audience, in reality the CRS report is essentially based on published reports and is not an assessment based on some classified documents available with the US State

Department or its intelligence agencies", he wrote. The CRS report had also said that in 2014 the Indian parliamentary election could see a stiff battle between Narendra Modi and Rahul Gandhi.

Among the BJP's likely candidates for the prime ministership in future elections in 2014 "is Gujarat Chief Minister Narendra Modi, who has overseen impressive development successes in his state, but who is also dogged by controversy over his alleged complicity in lethal anti-Muslim rioting there in 2002", the CRS report had said. Curiously from BJP's point of view, the report analysed that the saffron party too has made changes in its approach and strategy "to be a formidable challenger in scheduled 2014 polls". "These include a more effective branding of the party as one focused on development and good governance rather than emotive, Hindutva-related issues, and Nitin Gadkari's success at quelling intra-party dissidence and, by some accounts, showing superior strategising and organising skills as compared to his predecessors".

***

On the development paradigm, statisticians swear that Gujarat accounts for five per cent of India's population but 16 per cent of its industrial output and as high as 22 per cent of its exports. Its growth rate is higher than the national figures and die-hard optimists already compare Modi's Gujarat, one-time supposedly the 'hate land' for anti-Muslim riots, with China's Gungadong province of the 1990s that had given China the extra-ordinary lead in manufacturing. Today, Gujarat has emerged as a hub of major industries including the centre of five major car makers.

Auto experts say car makers namely, Tata Motors, French car-maker Peugeot, General Motors and Ford have hit the road to Modi-land largely due to power availability and port connectivity. While some people are already calling Gujarat, 'the Detroit of the East', Modi himself twitted describing his state as Asia's auto hub.

These contradictions of Gujarat being hailed as the industrial locomotive for the country on one hand and also being run down for harbouring an intolerant society with the Chief Minister at the receiving end of serious allegations thus remain the principal theme of this book. Along with these, what has been deservedly analysed in details is Modi's not so secret ambition in national politics.

Talking objectively, Modi, titled the 'Hindu *Hridaysamrat'* (Ruler of a Hindu heart) has over the last decade truly weathered enough brickbats and political discomfort. Most of these are his own making and the remaining is due to the highly communal frenzy in Gandhi's Gujarat and to a great extent the obsession of a section of media and social workers to find fault with Modi and the Gujarat government for everything.

There's no denying that Modi is the Chief Minister of a state; wherein the 'Kalinga phenomenon' has not dawn on the Hindus after indiscriminate looting and the killing of the Muslims in 2002. Unlike Emperor Ashoka, who moved by the slaughter of humans turned to non-violence and spread Buddhism after seeing the mass destruction in Kalinga War; among Hindus in Gujarat – and that include Gujaratis and importantly non-Gujaratis too – there was no sense of remorse.

While everyone makes a big issue of Modi being singularly responsible for the hyper communal image of Gujarat, a deeper analysis of the socio-political puzzles reveal that in a way Modi is also just being 'led'. If Modi is a pragmatic politician, how can he be faulted? After all, which Chief Minister can go against the overwhelming near 90 per cent voice of his people? Look at what Manipur Chief Minister did in disallowing Naga rebel leader Thuingaleng Muivah from visiting his native village?

I call this phenomenon the 'collaboration' of the state with communal organisations. Modi is simply playing back to the gallery.

So much has been Modi's success in these endeavours that one-time Hindutva zealot Pravin Togadia has been forced into oblivion after a failed battle of wits with Narendra Modi. Gujarat watchers see much bigger games behind all these. While Modi and BJP are in power for more than last ten years in Gujarat, a key frontal organisation of the Sangh, the VHP has been rendered rather into playing a second fiddle if not totally out of scene.

The Chief Minister has not only sidelined Togadia, who had taken a very aggressive stance against Advani's 'Jinnah secular' remarks; but the VHP's "good works" in the state too have been forgotten.

Prior to the Modi phenomenon in Gujarat, the VHP used to call the shots. Even post-Godhra bandh on February 28, 2002 was called by VHP and BJP had only faithfully toed the Sangh organisational line. And what followed the rest is history. The VHP supported Modi wholeheartedly during the 2002 assembly elections, Modi's *Gaurav Yatra* prior to the polls that year had the backing of VHP foot soldiers. But since then Modi has chosen to ignore and sideline the VHP and its leaders, especially the one-time vocal Pravin Togadia.

In 2005, Gordhan Zadafia, one-time Modi confidant, had refused to take oath as minister ostensibly at the instance of Togadia and former BJP stalwart, Keshubhai Patel. It's on this backdrop, we must see how former BJP strategist Govindacharya is campaigning against Modi and how Modi's home minister of 2002, Gordhan Zadafia has floated a regional party and charges Modi with corruption and at the same time swears by the ideals of RSS.

The state's principal opposition Congress is also trying to play back to the audience without offering itself as a viable 'secular' alternative. While Sonia Gandhi's party goes overboard in appeasing Muslims and also pinning the Sangh Parivar for Malegaon and Hyderabad blasts, it has turned to an ex-RSS man Shankersinh Vaghela to take on Modi.

The party's best known RSS-baiter Digvijaya Singh has maintained a studied silence on it. However, we have a microscopic case wherein Manishankar Aiyar, a known Sonia-confidant, who has spoken against Congress going with 'soft secularism' in Gujarat.

The party at times is not going strictly by the books to fight Modi. The Lokayukta issue is a controversy which can be seen in that perspective wherein Congress had sought to make suitable and selective use if not misuse of the office of the Governor to its benefit and to embarrass the Modi regime. Is the Modi camp entirely wrong when it says that Congress is trying to get rid of Modi from the throne of Gandhinagar by backdoor – the use of Lokayukta office?

Now this element of polarisation has gone beyond a point. No longer, it is merely on religious plane. These days in Gujarat, it is rightly rumoured that there are two sets of people – one who approve of Narendra Modi and the other, albeit in minority, who do not. The three-day *Sadbhavna* Fast by the Gujarat Chief Minister from September 17, 2011 brought that to clear focus, with an explicit message that Modi is eyeing beyond Gujarat.

By trying to focus on the 'Gujarat's development model' for a prosperous India, he has made his intentions clear. Many suggest, unlike the past the Gujarat Chief Minister is now even ready to take on the party's central leadership. In a way, he is already seen as being pitted against his one-time mentor and a great benefactor LK Advani.

One wonders, why and how he decided to stay away from the BJP national executive meet in Delhi in September 2011. Modi cited the reason of Navaratri for missing the mega event wherein top BJP leaders pilloried the UPA government for gross 'infighting within the cabinet' and the corruption. Top leaders like Sushma Swaraj predicted mid-term polls; a sentiment endorsed by LK Advani and Arun Jaitley. On the other hand, BJP could not pose a united face due to Modi's absence.

Contrary to BJP's official explanation, the general interpretation was that Modi stayed away from the national executive meet in Delhi as he is not too happy with party's decision to invite Bihar Chief Minister Nitish Kumar to flag off Advani's Rath Yatra.

If at all, Modi is today pitted against LK Advani for the prime ministerial candidate for BJP though the party has ruled out naming one for the time being, the relationship between the two Hindutva mascots has come a full circle. On September 12, 2011, when the Supreme Court refused to allow filing chargesheet or FIR against Modi for Ehsan Jafri murder, there was rumour-mongering that BJP's second generation leaders in Delhi – including Jaitley and Sushma Swaraj – would now prop up Advani as a natural claimant for the top job.

Having said these, it ought to be mentioned here that this is not for the first time that there is an attempt to push Modi for the prime ministerial candidate. Within a month since his historic victory in 2002 polls, Modi was invited by BJP's Mumbai unit on January 12, 2003 for a felicitation function. But the occasion was blissfully designed to rechristen him as the BJP's latest brand equity. If Modi's larger than life cutouts and three kilometers banner complimenting his poll victory and accolades from key leaders like Gopinath Munde were any indication, it was clear that one-time backroom strategist of the party had emerged on the national scene as 'Mr Durable'.

Modi's ambition was dominant even then. He himself prescribed a bigger role for himself when in his spirited speech he had announced that like his Mumbai visit he would tour all Congress-ruled states to give the respective Congress Chief Ministers a run for their money. "After all, fourteen Chief Ministers came together to campaign against me (for December 2002 polls)", Modi had said in his characteristic style urging the crowd not to be apologetic about Hindutva.

"*Kasa kai.... Kem chho....* Mein yeanh Vilasrao ki khabar lene aya hoon. "How are you all? I am in Mumbai today to enquire about Vilasrao Deshmukh's health", he had said to thunderous applause from the crowd. Modi had refused to equate party's victory in Gujarat as victory of Hindutva alone, saying, "Hindutva is always unaffected by BJP's victory or loss. Hindutva *ajay hae* (it is immortal)".

Like most reporters at the Shivaji Park near Dadar junction, an otherwise known citadel of Shiv Sena supremo Bal Thackeray, I too was impressed with the kind of response Modi had evoked. In my dispatch, therefore, I did report dutifully: "Narendra Modi has arrived! Stepping out of his fiefdom Hindu laboratory Gujarat, Narendra Modi on Sunday evening (Jan 12, 2003) took leap for the first time to test ground as neo-Hindu Hridaysamrat......" (*The Free Press Journal*, Jan 13, 2003).

Not surprisingly, emboldened by the tremendous turnout to Modi bash, BJP leader Gopinath Munde asserted that the saffron party was too eager to repeat the 'Gujarat pattern' in Maharashtra and challenged the then Chief Minister Vilasrao Deshmukh to dissolve the state assembly and face the people. However, BJP's attempts to replicate Modi magic had failed in Himachal Pradesh as the party was ousted only a few months later.

So much has been Modi's pervasive influence that within months after locking horns with the Gujarat Chief Minister, on 22 January, 2012, BJP president Nitin Gadkari sought to buy peace with Modi and rather in a surprising gesture favoured beleaguered Gujarat Chief Minister for the top job. He also promised to back his candidature as party chief. "I will never be a candidate for PM nor will I topple anybody. Modi has good potential to be BJP president and PM", he had told the television news channel *Headlines Today*. But all these relate to Gadkari's shadow boxing with Modi as he appointed a known Modi-dislike Sanjay Joshi as in-charge of UP affairs of the party. The Gujarat Chief Minister had declined to campaign for the party for the crucial polls in UP in February 2012.

On February 26, 2012, none other than Arun Jaitley, someone who enjoys good rapport with Modi, admitted that there were serious differences within the party over the responsibility given to Sanjay Joshi though he tried to delink the fact that Modi refused to campaign due to the same.

"There could be differences of opinion on what responsibility should be given to a person. But this has got nothing to do with Modi not campaigning in UP elections", Jaitley said when asked whether Modi's decision to boycott the UP campaign stemmed from his anger with Gadkari over Joshi's appointment.

Sanjay Joshi, a formerly RSS points man in BJP headquarter, was ousted from the party following a CD of him purportedly with a woman surfaced in December 2005 during the party's national executive meet in Mumbai. In fact, even senior party leader LK Advani reportedly disapproved of Gadkari's decision to install Joshi as in-charge of UP polls.

Sanjay Joshi, a Brahmin from Maharashtra, was believed to be an organisational worker who believed in creating good relations with workers at the grassroots level.

Both Joshi and Modi shared good relation in the earlier days. However, rivalry started with both of them stealing the limelight. BJP insiders say there was another pretext for Modi deciding to stay away as the saffron party did not want to oblige Congress by polarising the voters in the crucial state where Congress was going all out to woo Muslims and also establish the bigger hold for their crown prince Rahul Gandhi.

Again in May 2012, Modi gave his nod for Nitin Gadkari's second consecutive stint as party president only after his *bete noire* Sanjay Joshi was forced to voluntary resign from the BJP national executive. Advani and Leader of the Opposition Sushma Swaraj stayed away from the party rally even as spokespersons like Ravi Shankar Prasad tried in vain to explain to journalists that they should not read too much into the two leaders' absence as they had other pre-occupations.

The headline hunter, as I have described earlier, that Modi is; was at his rhetoric best trying to hit out at

Manmohan Singh-led UPA. By then, undoubtedly, he had taken the centrestage. "The Gujarat Chief Minister, with a known penchant for plucking catch-phrases from the contemporary events", as a report ran in *The Telegraph,* took pot shot the Congress-led dispensation describing the UPA as a Nirmal Baba durbar.

The self-proclaimed godman, Nirmal Baba, who has connections with Bengal and Jharkhand, was recently caught allegedly cheating and committing fraud on his adherents. He is accused of using quick-fix panaceas like swallowing rosogollas to treat ailments, said the report.

"You must have seen lots of his shows on TV. Nirmal Baba says eat a rosogolla and earn a reprieve for your sins. This government too said (in 2009), elect us to power and we will bring down prices in 100 days. Didn't they say it?" Modi asked a packed rally at the Kamgar Stadium in Mumbai.

Modi's reference was to the UPA report card released on the occasion of completion of its three years in office wherein the government talks highly about one per cent growth in agricultural production, from 2.5 to 3.5 per cent. "What kind of a report card is this? Gujarat, which until ten years ago suffered seven droughts in ten years, recorded an agrarian growth of 11 per cent", Modi said to a thunderous applause including from Gadkari.

However, besides Sushma Swaraj and Advani staying away from the rally, Arun Jaitley, party's chief parliamentary strategist and Leader of the Opposition in Rajya Sabha, also left as soon as he was done with his speech and before Narendra Modi spoke. Notably, Jaitley-Modi friendship goes to 2002 days when as the Union Minister Jaitley had time and again come to the defence of Modi. But all these do not imply about smooth sail for BJP. "Has the BJP preserved its unity? Not quite", wrote veteran columnist and longtime BJP watcher Rajinder Puri in *The Statesman,* May 27, 2012.

"…. both LK Advani and the Lok Sabha's Leader of the Opposition, Sushma Swaraj, were conspicuously absent (at BJP rally in Mumbai). Excuses trotted out about previous engagements may be conveniently trashed. The Leader of the Opposition in the Rajya Sabha, Arun Jaitley, attended the rally but left before Modi spoke. Later in the day, Jaitley in a public statement while criticising the UPA government openly invited West Bengal Chief Minister Mamata Banerjee to quit the UPA and join the NDA. This unconventional public invitation is pregnant with meaning. It indicates the future course of action that will likely be followed by the Advani supporters. If Modi can bully the RSS so can Advani. To find the soft spot for hitting Modi and Gadkari was easy and obvious. Inviting Mamata Banerjee was the giveaway. Mamata cannot alienate the minority vote. She would join only if Modi was marginalised or even eliminated. The same holds true for other NDA leaders like Nitish Kumar and Sharad Yadav. One wonders if the RSS had calculated that. Projecting Narendra Modi as the prime ministerial candidate and the main vote-getter implies that the BJP would be prepared to go it alone and strive for a single party majority. Advani and his supporters would rule out that option and stick with the NDA as the future alternative. Thanks to the RSS, the BJP has sharpened a split personality. How will the party swing? Will it remain united or split?" Rajinder Puri wrote.

***

No one in 2002 could conceive of a Gujarat – riding high on the wave of Hindu fanaticism as well as high growth path – as it has been put on such a roadmap by Modi. Similarly, in 2004, when NDA was voted out of office in a "fractured mandate" as Advani later described; no one had conceived of a politician in Advani – post-2005 - so much afflicted with failure and indecisiveness and perhaps also a few wrong decisions. Paradoxically, today, Advani needs his one-time protégé Narendra Modi more than the other. Modi rules

Gujarat and Advani's political constituency Gandhinagar is Modi's citadel.

As a master strategist of his own political roadmap, Modi, most of the time is in his elements choosing the words carefully and correctly. In the *Sadbhavna* Fast, though he stuck to his pet 'parochial Gujarati' slogan of 'six crore Gujaratis', he also tried to offer himself as a politician in search of 'reconciliation'. Modi told the gathering on the last day of his fast that "my government has not done anything for minority or even for majority. Whatever the Gujarat government does, we do it for all". These are really more than good rhetoric of a time-tested politician.

In many ways, one presumes, Modi's relationship with Muslims illustrates a peculiar combination of triumph and tragedy. Much has been, predictably, written and spoken about Modi's refusal to wear a Muslim skullcap offered to him at the venue by an Imam. The Congress leaders and other Modi baiters suggested that by his action the Gujarat Chief Minister, who has tried to make a changeover in his image had his mask slipped off. Gandhinagar-based local artiste Mallika Sarabhai, also a known Modi critic, said by the episode "his real face had emerged". Renuka Chowdhary, Congress spokesperson, was articulate enough to say, *"Modiji logon ko topi pehnate hain, apne aap pehente nahin* (Modi fools others; he does not get fooled himself".

However, the Gujarat watchers for many years say, contrary to the criticism that the Gujarat Chief Minister did not make use of *Sadbhavna* (Goodwill) Fast if he meant so genuinely; mere indication of his search for 'reconciliation' was no small move. According to this school of thought, it was a 'brave gesture' and a calculated risk for a Chief Minister facing the electorate of Gujarat in 2012 - at least two years before Modi is really catapulted as the prime ministerial candidate for BJP in 2014 polls.

Their argument being: Gujarat is so much biased even among common citizenry towards the Hindutva philosophy that Congress too has turned back to a former RSS pracharak

Shankersinh Vaghela to take on Modi. In 2002 too, Vaghela was the Congress supposed 'bulldog' to fight Modi but had failed miserably.

Over the years now, Modi's personal life has been consumed much by his politics and administration. In many ways, he embodies a neo-assertiveness of Gujarati community, known for their entrepreneurship and the acumen of 'Baniya class', ruling the state with a neo-authority and also fighting New Delhi -- that is the Central Government. From time to time, he is also discharging his role single-handedly and authoritatively that he can be easily mistaken as a 'dictator'.

On his own part, Modi says, "The last decade has come to be known as the decade of development for Gujarat. The reason for this can be attributed to the age-old philosophy that political stability breeds public confidence and hence translates to inclusive development for the state".

On his part, yet again even his ardent critics would agree that Modi has successfully read the pulse of people of Gujarat. In 2011-12, on way to the polls for scoring a hat-trick at the assembly polls, he did try to eye beyond his pocket-burrow state of Gujarat and look for wider acceptability nationwide. But he stuck well to the BJP's core value of many years: no appeasement for Muslims or others. This also forms his strengths rather than the rhetoric of the development. "This keeps him on the winning side. The younger generation both in Gujarat and outside Gujarat will endorse this", agreed an enthusiastic Muslim supporter at his three-day *Sadbhavna* Fast.

"We have to look beyond 2002. Look at what the Left Front did in Bengal to Muslims in the name of secularism. The young Hindus and Muslims believe that Gujarat has risen above petty politics and sectarian divide and chosen the path of inclusive development", one Rahmati Ali has been quoted as saying at the fast venue.

A net savvy Christian gentleman is also reported to have written in a social networking site: "Modi is correct. All are equal in the eyes of law. It is only a system of equitable benefits that can help India develop. Real culprits who brought the communal divide are Congress and opportunist Communists".

I know of Congress cabinet ministers in Delhi who not quite surprisingly say that it is the development in Gujarat, which ensured Modi's popularity and not the pro-Hindutva image.

Another broad area that has been examined rather minutely is the limitation of the Modi brand. Any concept of politicians behaving like saints in a selfless manner is simply senseless. Modi's fast and speeches were therefore clearly tailor-made to suit his mission - compartmentalised into two categories - Gujarat assembly polls in 2012 and also the shot for prime ministership in 2014.

In this endeavour, he has been well-supported by BJP's top brass especially LK Advani. The effort only got a major booster with the presence of Akali chief Parkash Singh Badal and two emissaries from Jayalalithaa at his *Sadbhavna* Fast. But things are still too early. Nitish Kumar-led JD(U), a principal NDA constituent, is still far from reconciling to the concept of agreeing to Modi's role in 2014 Lok Sabha polls.

Advani would definitely be in the race as he has repeatedly declined to opt out voluntarily. JD(U) chief Sharad Yadav mocked at the *Sadbhavna* Fast, while the party spokesman Shivanand Tiwari recalled Modi's failure to deliver 'Raj Dharma' as was assigned by Atal Behari Vajpayee - that is protect minorities in 2002.

A section of BJP leaders privately admit about the limitations of Modi brand in national politics. Though hyped more than once, Modi has failed to ensure victory for BJP candidates outside Gujarat.

Congress leader Shankersinh Vaghela, who also sat on a counter fast in September, 2011, rightly said, "Wherever Modi campaigned in 2009, BJP lost". Many see pragmatism in this analysis.

Advani's rejection in 2009 was due to hard-line Hindutva image as compared to Vajpayee's pan-Indian acceptability. Modi campaigned even in Assam assembly polls in 2011, but the result was failure. Even in Gujarat, BJP's performance in both Lok Sabha polls - 2004 and 2009 were not good. The message perhaps is: Gujaratis too could prefer Modi and BJP only at the state level but not in the same manner at the national level. Thus, the moot question still is: Can Modi emerge as a vote-catcher nationwide?

The refrain among BJP leaders, albeit on the condition of anonymity, is that to ensure Modi as prime minister of India, the pan-India voter should turn pro-Hindutva (read communal) like in Gujarat. This looks unlikely as even majority Hindus outside Gujarat hardly endorse post-Godhra riots and indiscriminate killings of the Muslims.

But BJP insiders also feel that both 2009 Lok Sabha polls and assembly elections in Assam in 2011 took place prior to the Supreme Court "reprieve" for Modi as also the latest report by a US research team that Gujarat is 'best administered' state in India.

None other than Advani has analysed these well. "Now, American lawmakers and the State Department are being primed for the return of the BJP to power in New Delhi, with Modi at the helm as prime minister".

Echoing this spirit, BJP strategists think they would campaign well to highlight these points to change the equations. Moreover, the optimists also believe that by 2014, if the Gujarat trial court gives its order with a clean chit to Modi, then the battle will be more than half won. But for BJP to return to power, the challenges are manifold and much beyond the Modi-prime minister-in-waiting debate.

The saffron party has to get into business of fetching more seats in states like Andhra Pradesh, West Bengal, Kerala, Odisha, the entire North East and partly Bihar. No one should dream of becoming prime minister or bringing a party into power in Delhi without acceptability in these states - totalling as many as 196 Lok Sabha seats.

BJP needs to put its house in order too. While, the BJP leadership largely thinks that the timing "suits" it for a mid-term poll as Congress and UPA are besieged with corruption, there's little realisation that corruption vis-à-vis Lokpal campaign has been hijacked from the opposition political parties by Anna Hazare. The former Finance Minister Yashwant Sinha has spoken about it already. In the words of Congress leader in-charge of Gujarat, Mohan Prakash: "the first impact of *Sadbhavna* Fast is, it led to cracks in NDA and BJP with JD(U) disapproving the fast altogether. The one-upmanship displayed by Modi has also unnerved many in BJP".

The developments in May 2012 on the eve and post-BJP national executive meet in Mumbai are only follow-up of these episodes.

In effect, the future prospects of BJP are more dependent on several conjectures. What impact Uttar Pradesh 2012 poll results would have? Can its one-time deserted leaders like Uma Bharati work together with leaders like Rajnath Singh and Kalraj Mishra remains to be seen? And what about its typical Congress-style of internal squabbling! The million dollar issue that needs to be settled is the debate on whether or not Modi as the prime minister of India would come only if BJP increases its tally in Lok Sabha significantly from the present humble 116.

In July 2011 issue the magazine *The Economist* said rather caustically, "so many things work properly in Gujarat that it hardly feels like India". In the run up to the 2009 Lok Sabha polls, which BJP after projecting LK Advani lost miserably, a large number of leading industrialists including Anil Ambani had said that Modi is the most potent prime minister material. So did Arun Shourie, then a party MP in the Rajya Sabha.

Taking a closer view on Modi's administration, I find there is logic in describing him as a 'part CEO' with prodigious management abilities, part a Hindutva poster boy. He could also be a part modern time revolutionary, who is helping to accommodate rural labour in growing manufacturing sector but in doing so, is he neglecting the core agriculture sector?

Gujarat's economy is to grow by double digits, even as India's rate slows to 7-8 per cent. I take a closer view on how and why the Congress and other detractors of Modi say development is essentially a process of survival of the Gujarati population given to immense talent in entrepreneurship and certain infrastructure advantages like the power and good ports.

Curiously, there are also several stories and allegations of crony capitalism and corruption as echoed by a former Modi aide Gordhan Zadafia and Congress leader Shaktisinh Gohil.

Besides, there is a critical analysis of development and displacement in Gujarat; wherein I try to debate on how and why in the past two decades, Gujarat has been losing agricultural land at a faster rate than it did between 1960 and 1980.

The compound annual growth of Gujarat's economy in 1990-91 to 1997-98 has been 8.99 per cent with the state showing good performance in accessing the benefits of new economic environment vis-à-vis the liberalisation. But in spite of these achievements, Gujarat has been suffering from certain weaknesses like low long-term growth in agriculture, low human development in terms of health, nutrition and education, degradation of natural resources and also regional disparity.

I have spoken about entrepreneurs' zeal of the Gujaratis. By this argument development is not entirely a new phenomenon in the state. As way back in 1980, 20 years after its creation and long before the Modi dispensation came on the scene; Gujarat was among the three fastest-growing states. In 1999-2000, its growth map equalled that of China. That means, Gujarat has maintained its growth chart even without Modi.

Another facet is the state's growing number of NRI strength. Apart from its long history of mercantilism, Gujarat, like Punjab, has a long history of migration abroad – even in the far-flung African countries besides the prosperous US, Canada and Europe.

The benefits from overseas did also result in rural prosperity and fuelled state's trade. But, it is also revealed that nearly 75 per cent of Other Backward Classes, Dalits and Adivasis, live in severe economic conditions. According to one estimate, Gujarat's production of cereals and other food grains in the industrialised phase of 1991-2001 declined to nearly half of what it was in 1990.

There was negative agricultural growth rate (decline) by 0.81 per cent between 1970s and 1980s as against 4.22 positive growths between 1960s and 1970s. Again, droughts in late nineties kept agricultural growth almost at stagnancy and this leaving a cascading impact as poor agro growth graph had resulted in adverse impact in nutrition and educational status of the poor and the marginalised sections. Therefore, it is not quite surprising that Jairam Ramesh, the Rural Development Minister under Dr Manmohan Singh, had this to state: "On nutrition, I am puzzled as to why a high rate of malnutrition continues to persist even in pockets of high economic growth like Gujarat".

A 2010 report by IFPRI, a US-based research organisation, put Gujarat among the five worst performing states in India in reducing hunger, along with Bihar, Madhya Pradesh, Chhattisgarh and Jharkhand, another report had claimed that in worker's wage share, Gujarat has fallen from 23 to eight per cent. So, who is really seeing the development in Gujarat? Modi's former home minister and now a critic Zadafia says, "Gujarat development is for Ambanis and the likes".

It goes without stating that Modi's problems are far from over. Development or no development, it is a bitter fact that Modi has given the Hindutva ideology a bad reputation – something rare in the civilisational history of Hinduism and India. The bottom line today is that: Narendra Modi and Sangh Parivar must stop telling directly or indirectly that what happened in the name of Godhra-train fire was right.

Until and unless, a civilisation or a political party is prepared to face up the truth; they can never have the credibility in true sense of the word.

I am not taking sides. If excessive Muslim appeasement has been a wrong, so is the excessive Hindutva assertion. The beauty of a garden is in the presence of wide range of flowers. Pluralism and mutual tolerance is India's strength for ages.

In this book, we would examine that the inherent strength of Indian civilisation and Hinduism is not properly appreciated by today's champions of Hindutva. What they are doing is only anti-thesis to Hinduism and not aimed at Hindu renaissance.

"Our civilisational history has followed no single chronology. I may not agree with many things in Hinduism. But it is never a one book religion", my late father-in-law, Sushil Kumar Deb, a former hardcore CPI-M man from Tripura, and a former teacher, had summed it up in around 2003.

He had explained that the richness of the civilisational values can be understood from the fact that Buddhism flourished more in Japan and East Asia than in north India or Nepal, where Buddha was born. The Japanese, Chinese and Thai tourists visit Buddhists holy sites in India, like Muslims visit Mecca and Christians go to Jerusalem, he had explained.

It's not purity or one-religion uniformity that has India as we know today - an emerging economy even after the holocaust of partition of 1947. The true strength of Indian nationhood is in its diversity.

The most underlining message from the fellow political class for Narendra Modi remains: while almost all allies of UPA are disillusioned with Congress, none of them even remotely has shown inclination yet to switch over to BJP-led NDA.

And if Modi wants to be India's prime minister, he has to pledge to uphold the same. It's not without good reason that we can take pride of the fact that more Muslims reside in India than in Pakistan, a country carved out of Mother India with the claim to offer a 'pious' land to the followers of Islam.

Chapter – 1

Narendra Modi
The Past and the Present

"Beloved, gaze in thine own heart,
The holy tree is growing there.....
Gaze no more in the bitter glass...
For there a fatal image grows
That the stormy night receives
Roots half hidden under snows"

- WB Yeats

About nine and half months after the Godhra carnage which had erupted Gujarat into unprecedented communal violence, elections were first held on December 12, 2002. Expectedly, it was country's most fiercely contested and keenly watched state assembly elections in recent times. Three days later on December 15, the counting of votes revealed that the people of Gujarat have voted overwhelmingly in favour of BJP and had endorsed Hindutva hardliner card with some sort of vengeance.

That same evening, not quite an unexpected thing also happened. None other than the then prime minister Atal

Behari Vajpayee endorsed the Hindutva theory or rather the Moditva, when he came out to join the enthusiastic BJP supporters at his official residence, 7 RCR (Race Course Road) in the national Capital. What perhaps surprised both his admirers and political adversaries was when Vajpayee did maintain that for BJP with Gujarat victory came a season of victories and that the party cadres should start working taking "*prerna* (inspiration)" from Gujarat. He had unofficially and perhaps also unknowingly crowned Modi as someone who could easily take over the reins from the duo of Vajpayee and Advani.

It is not without good reason that at the swearing-in ceremony a few days later at spacious Sardar Patel stadium in Ahmedabad had banners reading 'Aayo re aayo, Gujarat ne sher aayo (Here comes Gujarat's Lion)' and 'Modi today CM, tomorrow PM of Hindu Rashtra'.

The writing was clear. Thus, Modi's high ambitions for prime ministership and something endorsed by his followers and party workers, is therefore, not a circa 2011 phenomenon.

This was the period which also marked modest but certain paradigm shift in the second generation of BJP leadership. Modi was then only 52, and therefore with the crucial pressure from the Sangh Parivar, the talk of paradigm shift towards the generation next only had gained currency. There were other factors in 2002 which went in his favour.

One primary reason was that he had the full-backing of LK Advani, who was till then the undisputed Hindutva poster boy and the 'Secular Jinnah' hara-kiri of 2005 had not yet taken place.

Till then, Narendra Modi was only a backroom strategist and who had delivered Gujarat to the party fold amid multi-pronged challenges. In the run up to the Gujarat polls, Modi as the chief campaigner and the chief minister in office had obviously overshadowed two giants LK Advani and Atal Behari Vajpayee.

Thanks to the polarisation, Modi not only helped BJP score a hat-trick to take control of the western border state – also known as Hindu laboratory – but its vote share reached a peak at 51 per cent followed by 44.8 per cent in 1998, 42.5 in 1995 and 26.7 in 1990.

Modi grew larger than life image as only a few months ago in August 2001 and February 2002, the party had faced a rather indifferent electorate among the same '*panch* crore Gujaratis'.

It was a neo-assertive Modi, who riding on the wave of 'Hindu consolidation' recorded a resounding victory even in Northern region and tribal belts of Panchmahals and Dahod showing post-Godhra riots had sought to bring even tribals and OBCs under the influence of Hindutva school of thought. BJP won Godhra, from where it all started, with Bajrang Dal stalwart Haresh Bhatt openly declaring that it was 'Hindutva' which bagged him the seat.

Prior to that before he was made the chief minister by an embattled BJP leadership replacing Gujarat old-hand Keshubhai Patel, as a general secretary Modi had failed to deliver states like Madhya Pradesh to his party. Thus, it was only after 2002 riots and the December 2002 elections that year - with much ease the vacant third slot in BJP hierarchy after Vajpayee and his deputy Advani went to Modi, may be. And there was no great competition unlike post 2004, after BJP lost the crucial Lok Sabha poll. Kalyan Singh, hero of Ram temple agitation, had already burnt his fingers by making personal attacks against Vajpayee and another RSS-favoured and the then Human Resource Development Minister Murli Manohor Joshi was also sidelined.

The results of Assembly elections of 2002 December also marked a beginning of talks about Gujarat formula elsewhere in the country. This simply also meant making Modi, the party's new vote catcher. None other than the then Prime Minister Vajpayee himself gave credence to these theories when in his characteristic mixed signals speech, he had said, "People wanted BJP and certainly not the negativism of Congress", and also posed a question whether 'Gujarat model' should be repeated elsewhere.

Not surprisingly, it was the same Vajpayee, who on 5 April, 2002, at Shah Alam relief camp speech in Ahmedabad had lamented at the anti-Muslims riots and wondered with "what face" he could go abroad.

But Modi's charismatic success did not necessarily mean a bed of roses all the way. A strong team of detractors has appeared from among the police force including the likes of one-time senior official at the coveted crime branch in Gandhinagar, Sanjiv Bhatt, and also Additional DGP, CID, RB Sreekumar. We will look into details on Sanjiv Bhatt's battle against Modi regime - going on constantly braving several odds.

Today, as we talk about Narendra Modi, one remembers a figure in him who also exemplifies the saying that not every noun needs adjectives. But he has a stock full of those.

Gujarat's 'new Lion', Gujarat's Gaurav or 'Pride of Gujarat', *Chhota Sardar,* a 'clean Chief Minister' and a 'CEO' on the positive realm, on the negativity the list is perhaps larger - a communal, rabble-rouser, a new Milosevic for Hindus and for Muslims a textbook case of a fascist, 'Nero' and many more.

Excited that he was able to establish himself at the helm of Gujarat affairs, his rise is an example of an adage that human life is full of miracles. One really will never know what miracle and pleasant surprises are stored in some people's life.

Sitting happy in his office as the Chief Minister of a growth-oriented state and also wondering how he has to shed the image of a 'Muslim hater', Modi in 2011 was perhaps counting his days for yet another date with electorate destiny - the next year's state assembly polls. On September 12, 2011, the Supreme Court provided him an opportunity to rekindle his dream when it rejected the plea to make him a co-accused in the Gulberg Society incidents of February 28, 2002.

Looking back, the political growth of the man has truly come as unpredictable as has been his metamorphosis into an accomplished *neta* from a humble boy from little known Mehsana - where Modi had turned RSS pracharak (roughly translated into a propagator) at the age of 22.

"I am an organisation man," he had said umpteen times in the last decade well-aware that like life, political career, is also full of miracles wherein much surprises - including pleasant and unpleasant ones - are often stored in.

"Necessity is the biggest driver in life and also a giver", he had remarked casually in 2002, a day after Akshardham temple was attacked in Gandhinagar. He could be banking on these 'surprise' factors of destiny; but a man of action that he is - Modi has kept himself eyeing for the national leadership without any hesitation or any ambiguity.

Till date, he has not ruled out such a possibility. He only says, I have not yet thought of these. "My mission in life is to give my best to the country; and I am trying that to the best of my ability", he had said in an interview.

I have spoken earlier about his ability to judge people's pulse; something he himself takes pride in rather openly. During 2002 days, when once I questioned him about his '*Hum panch hamare pachis*' remark attributed to Muslims' largely; his reply was cryptic: "I know people's pulse... I have never said Muslims. It was a comment on family planning and people of Gujarat liked and endorsed what I said". True to somewhat like Vajpayee characteristic, Modi was only telling half-truth and that too very cleverly.

It's true, the people of Gujarat really endorsed his comments against unstructured family life of the Muslims, but Modi was concealing the obvious fact that the target of his tirade was the battered minority community only.

Modi faced serious challenges to his post from intra-party rivals led by veteran Keshubhai Patel more than once. First was in April 2002, when the BJP national executive meet held at Goa and where the BJP leadership rejected his 'faulty offer' of resignation reportedly much owing to Advani's backing and against Vajpayee's original plans.

The second – and a stronger threat came in 2004 after BJP lost the crucial Lok Sabha polls. However, he successfully braved through the challenges reportedly after his camp threatened to quit the saffron party. The BJP's diagnosis was apt that it was the overwhelming negative publicity especially among the minorities that cost BJP and also the other NDA constituents badly. But the saffron party, albeit under determined backing of the likes of LK Advani, Arun Jaitley and of course the RSS, could not show him the doors. It's due to the electorate debacle of 2004 that makes Nitish Kumar so blatantly angry against Modi. Nitish Kumar, JD(U)'s party strength in Lok Sabha had nose-dived to half-a-dozen as against the immense success of Kumar's bitter rival Lalu Prasad-led RJD and also by Ram Vilas Paswan.

It's to Nitish Kumar's credit since 2005 assembly polls in Bihar, the 2009 Lok Sabha polls and again the 2010 Bihar assembly polls that both his rivals Lalu Prasad and Paswan are sidelined into the periphery of Bihar politics.

In November 2011, I had interviewed Ram Vilas Paswan wherein he admitted that his decision to quit NDA was solely because BJP had not conceded to pressure from allies like his to replace Modi.

(Interview excerpts)

Q: You seem to be targeting the BJP government in Gujarat also. People see this as your desperation to look for lost secular space in Bihar and the national polity.

Paswan: I am not speaking against the BJP and RSS for the first time. I have always raised my voice against the Hindu terror menace. I quit the Vajpayee government in 2002, a day before my trip to China, over Gujarat.

Q: Tell us more about your resignation from the NDA government. That probably sowed the seeds for the floating of the UPA at a later stage.

Paswan: I resigned from the ministry when my suggestion to ask for the resignation of Narendra Modi was not heeded by BJP leaders. I had also suggested that the NDA government issue a resolution condemning the violence against Muslims and said that the Lok Sabha express concern on the situation. This was also rejected. Then I cited the illustration of the 1970s when, during the Janata regime, as a ruling Janata Party member, I had moved a resolution expressing concern on attacks on Dalits. There was no division on it as Morarjibhai (then Prime Minister) said the government agreed with the resolution. Sometimes, you have to take tough decisions. The NDA leaders declined.

(November 19, 2011, The Statesman)

Denial of US Visa

Modi generates the element of dislike if not hatred not only from the Indian political class. In 2005, the US created a history of its own when it denied visa to the elected Chief Minister of Gujarat. The American official explanation for the same was that Modi and his government was "responsible for or directly carried out, at any time, particularly severe violations of religious freedom".

The UPA government of Manmohan Singh strongly protested over the move and the Prime Minister himself made a *suo-motu* statement on the floor of Parliament castigating the decision and said eloquently that whatever is being said about Modi are 'mere allegations'.

The argument holds water as no court of law had indicted Modi personally though the Supreme Court had allowed transfer of Best Bakery case out of Gujarat and also lamented that when Rome (read Gujarat) was burning, modern Neros were sleeping.

The Supreme Court had observed: "The modern day Neros were looking elsewhere when Best Bakery and innocent children and helpless women were being burnt and were probably deliberating how the perpetrators of the crime can be saved or protected". The apex court referring to acquittal of the accused of Best Bakery case (in a Vadodara court) had observed caustically, such acquittals were "unmerited, based on tainted evidence, tailored investigation, unprincipled prosecution and perfunctory trial and evidence".

There were angry editorials in Indian media and also there were a few individuals who took up the cudgel against the US decision for not granting visa to Modi. However, the Congress party was apparently not happy with the Prime Minister going 'over board' with his reaction and there were leaked reports that the Ministry of External Affairs then held under a Sonia Gandhi-protégé Natwar Singh too was not consulted for the Prime Minister's statement.

In the process of denying the diplomatic visa and also cancellation of a tourist visa, said '*The Indian Express*' in its editorial on March 19, 2005 the US administration had "allowed Modi not only to affect the genuine outrage of the persecuted but also to legitimately divert the spotlight from his own earned notoriety to US hypocrisies on issues of religious freedom". The daily pointed out that in its sharp display of 'double standards', the US had in the past played 'host' to the armed conspirators of Khalistan.

Such allegations and even dictatorship also hardly bothered the US as time and again, Washington had been pumping in huge amount for countries like Pakistan even under military ruler Gen Pervez Musharraf, under whose regime ISI complicity in Afghanistan too was somewhat a common knowledge.

Many seem to endorse the view that such a stance was taken by a country like the United States where the word 'Muslim' is routinely seen as a terrorist and post 9/11 even helpless Sikhs were mistaken as Muslims and were attacked.

"..... I do not see how such actions (denial of visa to Modi) will help bridge the divide between communities. The US should demonstrate its good intentions through examples such as by changing the anti-Muslim feeling within its own society or by developing kinder relations based on equality with Muslims of the world", wrote RK Singh, a former scientist with TIFR and a citizen of the US in a piece to '*The Indian Express*' (March 24, 2005).

However, there was other extreme view too. Actress Nafisa Ali, also a Congress party worker, argued that, "..... There is (was) a substantial Indian mainstream that is (was) delighted at Modi's embarrassment. I am one of them and hope that more follows. Even as my mind says that visa should be granted, my intellect and my heart rejoice (at the visa denial)".

On his part, Modi reacted by offering a red carpet welcome to the Florida Governor. "Gujarat will make efforts to welcome him and show him what love and hospitality means", Modi had said in his satellite message to Indian Associates in the United States. Modi was addressing the Asian-American Hotel Owners Association at Fort Lauderdale in Florida via satellite from his residence in Gandhinagar. Similarly, he addressed another such gathering of the Indian-American community at Madison Square Garden, New Jersey via satellite. But Modi has truly come a long way. Notwithstanding the views of the US administration in 2005, the US Congress study group has welcomed his developmental initiatives in 2011.

Most give the credit for Gujarat's monumental developmental works singularly to Modi because he has helped achieve what was impossible even a few years back - and is still difficult in several other states across India. Doing business is a hassle-free phenomenon in Gujarat today devoid of red-tapism.

Ron Somers, head of an American trade group, in one such conclave under the title 'Vibrant Gujarat' called Modi a progressive leader. Michael Kadoorie, a Hong Kong billionaire and chairman of the Asian Power Company, CLP Group hugged him in public and in his speech lauded Gujarat as being an even playing field. "I would encourage you all to invest here", he had said.

Bombardier, the Canadian company, built a manufacturing plant in Savli, to role out compartments for Delhi Metro in what is said to be a record 18 months. There are many others including Indian honchos Tatas and Ambanis. Thus when it comes to his administration and encouragement to entrepreneurship, he is no longer hated.

The results are also showing, say Gujarat government officials. In 2001, the year Modi took over office, Gujarat's economy shrank by five per cent and by 2011, and the state Gross Domestic Product shot up to an annual 11 per cent. In yet another turning point to boost Gujarat's industrialisation situation, on 29 October, 2011 in New Delhi, auto-maker Maruti Suzuki's board meeting approved a new manufacturing facility in Gujarat and purchase of land in Mehsana district. The board "granted approval to purchase land in district Mehsana for future expansion of manufacturing facilities. This purchase would be subject to final negotiations on price and all legal formalities being completed", a company announcement said. This was after Maruti's plant faced labour related problems in Haryana.

To his credit, the energy companies Royal Dutch Shell and Total have opened a major liquid natural gas terminal in Gujarat, and Indian Torrent Power has built a huge plant.

Among others, Tata Motors, DuPont, General Motors, Hitachi and dozens of other foreign and Indian companies have built factories, expanded operations and invested in projects in the state. "If you are an investor in India, Gujarat must be at the top of your list", said one business leader of an American trade group at a Vibrant Gujarat meet.

In effect, the business houses including those from outside these days hardly bother about media campaign and constant allegations from his detractors about 2002 carnage and Modi's supposed RSS-agenda, the 'hate Muslim' philosophy. Both the overseas and Indian corporate honchos laud his quick delivery system.

The compromise about his so-called communal credential and alleged inaction during 2002 riots or even ill-action later like Sohrabuddin encounter episode are small 'prices' to efficient and quick delivery mechanism.

One retired Gujarat cadre bureaucrat told me that Modi is used to "a neo-management and near-Hitler kind approaches to developmental works". "When some business magnate enters his office, Modi is prepared with a list of yes and nos to the possible questions. Most concerned secretaries of related projects are already summoned in his office with their goals and decisions almost decided. A fan of gizmos, Modi also uses IT revolution and most permit related matters are online. He expects his ministers and bureaucrats to perform with Godspeed", he had said.

In 2009, Gujarat attracted more planned investment than any other state in the country and about $ 54 billion by value of announced plans, according to business chamber ASSOCHAM. In effect, many say, there is a dearth of quick decision-making politician and that too with no tag of corruption; and this is where Modi has left his detractors shell-shocked. "When corporate houses and common people find an effective politician who can make things happen on the ground, they are willing to ignore certain flaws. Communalism is not such a big vice given the reputation of Indian *netas*", echoed a serving official.

Modi's admirers say, it is this delivery ability that makes his rivals nervous and at the same time spark off certain rows. In 2011, China's ambassador to India, Zhang Yan, reached out to Modi and expressed China's interest in working together to sharpen Gujarat's industrial and manufacturing edge. He also invited Modi to visit China, which the Chief Minister had accepted.

"The Chinese invitation to Modi is an astute political move, and sends a very strong political signal, particularly in the context of the fact that Modi was in 2005 controversially denied a visa to travel to the US for his role in the 2002 riots – on the strength of lobbying by human rights activists in the US", said a web newsletter from 'Gujarat-GujaratIndia.com'.

By rolling out the red carpet for Modi, in contrast to the US visa snub, Chinese officials are making a calculated investment in the future, which they know will be well received by a leader who prides himself as an embodiment of Gujarati *asmita* (self-respect), it said.

And unlike US diplomats, who (WikiLeaks cables reveal) said they were sending Modi "a clear message regarding the US government's concerns for the state of human rights and religious freedom in Gujarat", the Chinese are open to doing business with him without offering lectures on human rights, the article further said.

For Chinese leaders, Modi's involvement in the 2002 riots and his response as an administrator since then, have parallels with a defining moment in Chinese history: the 1989 massacre of students around the Tiananmen Square in Beijing.

Right after the 4th June, 1989 crackdown, China faced international criticism and was subjected to sanctions. Foreign investors, who had been warming up to the China story after the first round of reforms unveiled by Deng Xiaoping in 1976, no longer wanted to be associated with a regime that had blood on its hands. It was a particularly grim moment for the Chinese Communist Party. Yet, Deng Xiaoping successfully changed the China narrative by unleashing a second round of reforms, which was the cue for investors to return, overlooking the taint of Tiananmen.

Similarly, Modi has managed in recent years to change the narrative about Gujarat away from the horrendous 2002 riots, the newsletter said. No wonder, under Modi today, Ahmedabad figures only behind two Chinese cities - Chengdu and Chongqing - on Forbes' list of 10 fastest-growing cities of the future.

The series of accolades that poured in for Modi was really unthinkable once. After the anti-Muslim riots, he was considered a political pariah by secularists and a key BJP ally Nitish Kumar does not want to be seen even photographed with him. Post-2004 Lok Sabha polls, he was almost a liability for his political party and even Vajpayee wanted him replaced. But with Gujarat's soaring economy, and apparently a Supreme Court reprieve on Ehsan Jafri case, things are gradually changing. BJP leaders give him credit for developmental works and removing red-tapes. Modi's posters were plastered on billboards throughout Gujarat during the investment summit meetings and also *Sadbhavna* Fast proclaiming the state's support not only for investment but for social programmes like support of girl child education, private-public partnership in health and agro revolution.

Modi works relentlessly to materialise some of these achievements. A 'single', separated from his wife decades back, he takes rest only for 4-5 hours. He has worked hard his graph and also done so quite cleverly.

In 2002, Modi posed himself as the protector of Gujarati Pride targeted even 'Mian Musharraf'. He had made his election battle a fight against age-old Muslim tyranny.

In 2007, he made a good synthesis of development mantra along with 'no appeasement' towards Muslims. He almost endorsed the questionable encounter of Sohrabuddin amid much media attacks and even vilification by rivals like Sonia Gandhi, who virtually called him a 'merchant of death (*maut ka saudagar*)'. It's altogether a different chapter that Modi had in fact benefited from such gross indiscriminate kind of remarks.

In the run up to the 2012 assembly polls, he talked about 'inclusive growth of Gujarat and Gujaratis'. The theme of his *Sadbhavna* Fast speech in September 2011 was, "I do nothing for minorities nor anything for majority (the Hindus)". His development card is for all Gujaratis, Modi emphasised.

As the senior journalist Prabhu Chawla says, "He (Modi) has ensured that he remained prime news on prime time for the most part of the year". If newsmaker is to attain the immortality in the pages of history; among the Indian *neta* class, undoubtedly Modi would be at the top.

He has well bypassed the past demagogues like Vishwanath Pratap Singh, who had played the caste card or even Indira Gandhi, who had invented the art of creating vote banks in Muslims, in Tamils and perhaps also in Punjabi Hindus - only to be vilified one day - by all these sections.

But as an administrator, Modi knows the art of modern management pretty well. When Tata's Nano project was hounded out of West Bengal in 2008, he knew there would be probable competitions among other states to accommodate Nano car factory. On October 3, 2008 when Tata Motors announced that they would be moving out of Singur, Ratan Tata reportedly received letters of invitation from four states. But Modi sent in an SMS which simply said 'Welcome to Gujarat'.

Ratan Tata, Chairman, Tata Sons, later commented "Narendra Modi promised me it would take a few days. And his few days meant only three days wherein in common business-administration parlance in any other state could mean at least couple of months minimum". Located 60 km from Ahmedabad, an 1100-acre plot in Sanand was passed on to Tata Motors by the Modi regime.

This piece of land where the Tata Motors' manufacturing unit came up in a record 14 months had belonged to the Anand Agriculture University for over a century. In three days the government acquired the land and passed it to Tatas and there were no protest or so.

Many other industrial houses today also agree that Gujarat is most amenable to investment and industrial growth. However, Modi's detractors and some inherent skeptics have their reasons to ask, whose development Modi is eyeing at? What's the cost the poor land owners in villagers are paying to make Narendra Modi a paragon of development and make his state hassle-free for businessmen and a 'development laboratory'?

As a journalist, I am watching Modi for over 14 years now, sometime from close range, mostly during the last 10 years from a distance.

There's a quirk of paradoxical twists in the tale about him. Just as we know about his 'Mia Musharraf' remarks especially in months immediately after the riots and in the run up to the 2002 polls, there is an element which draws somewhat parallelism between him and Pervez Musharraf. Like Musharraf, Modi too was extremely obsessed about his image - when he seized power, when he oversaw the turbulent 2002 days of arson and killings and in the later stage as he tried to give a 'façade' of developmental governance to his state. Those who have kept a closer observation on him, admit, that Modi wanted to present himself palatable (acceptable) to various constituencies without, however, compromising on his chief plank - the hardcore Hindutva. Like Musharraf remained ever defensive of military role, Modi too has never compromised on his image as the Hindutva poster boy.

Like Musharraf, Modi also has been trying to build up his image to the international community and has so far suitably made use of the development in the state pretty well - definitely surpassing the attempts made by Musharraf.

But it would not be fair to label Modi as an image reflection of Musharraf. The former Pakistani ruler remained a pariah to most countries, Modi is somehow not. His Vintage Gujarat business summits are a pointer for the same as was his high-profile visit to China - essentially aimed to boost business.

Mainly to his detractors and also those who would like to be participating in resurgent Gujarat movement but do not approve of his 2002 polity of will full inaction, tolerating Modi is like the case of seeing an insect on a god statue - you cannot let it sit peacefully nor hurl stone at it.

Narendra Modi's image building exercise 'Vibrant Gujarat' too is well-planned. Like the one in 2011, he ensured that it was well-attended including by the likes of Ratan Tata, Ambani brothers, Gautam Adani and Anand Mahindra among the desi business honchos as well as the ambassadors of Japan and Canada - the two countries who signed as the 'official partners' for the mega event. There was also the Prime Minister of Rawanda Bernard Bakuza and the President of the US-India Business Council Rom Sommers.

The 'Vibrant Gujarat' has been successfully marketed as a major global business event every alternate year essentially to showcase the Chief Minister than perhaps the state. Nevertheless the impact is so profound that Modi's American lobbying and public relations firm, APCO Worldwide, also has bagged international awards for its work promoting the project.

So much is the aura or awe associated with Modi that many laurels coming from industry captains could even outdo best of political sycophancy of the Congress or Mayawati cult.

On the summit in 2011, at the glittering function in Gandhinagar on January 12, 2011, the Reliance group Chairman Mukesh Ambani said, "Gujarat is emerging as a superpower of the 21st century under him". His brother Anil Ambani further said, "After Mahatma Gandhi, it is under the leadership of Modi that the state is seeing a phenomenal progress. My father Dhirubhai Ambani, after meeting Mr Modi, had said he will go a long way". Tata group Chairman Ratan Tata too was all praise for the Chief Minister. "By your exemplary leadership, you are establishing new grounds in industrial development," he had said.

Officials in Gandhinagar say, the five summits since 2003 have generated investment pledges worth over $900 billion for Gujarat even as debate persists on how much money has really seen the ground of Gujarat and how much of it has been really transformed into projects. Nevertheless, on papers at least the 2011 show itself earned an assurance of over $ 450 billion.

But Modi's harmonious relation with the Indian corporate world did not start on a gold platter on its own. In fact, he had to struggle for it braving initial hiccups including very harsh words from known captains of the industry.

Deepak Parekh, the CEO of HDFC Bank, is one person who had already lamented over the riots and observed that India had lost its face as a secular country overseas. Narayana Murthy of Infosys and Azim Premji of Wipro had also condemned the violence.

In one Confederation of Indian Industry (CII) meet in New Delhi on February 6, 2003, Modi was rebuffed when Adi Godrej urged him to make use of people's mandate (2002 December poll results) to ensure safety and security of the citizens, something the then Prime Minister Atal Behari Vajpayee had urged Modi to uphold 'Raj Dharma' in April 2002.

Rahul Bajaj went more outspoken when he said, "Why don't we get investment in Kashmir, the North East, or Uttar Pradesh and Bihar? It is not just the lack of infrastructure, but also the sense of insecurity. I hope this won't happen in Gujarat". Modi shot back at the industry captains, "Others have vested interest in maligning Gujarat. What is your interest?" The Gujarat Chief Minister had gone back to his strongest pitch - the Gujarati pride - even as he invited the top honchos to visit his state.

"You and your pseudo-secular friends can come to Gujarat if you want an answer. Talk to my people. Gujarat is the most peaceful state in the country", he had said.

The ignominy for the Gujarat's '*sher* (lion)' could be understood as one Oxford-based historian and activist Jairus Banaji took on Modi at a function in Mumbai.

Observers say Modi was hurt at the developments. Back home on his return to Gandhinagar, his office had issued a statement pooh-poohing the corporate flak and said when the industry captains like Rahul Bajaj and Godrej questioned the state's law-and-order at a Confederation of Indian Industry (CII) conference in New Delhi, from the dais, he (Modi) could not tolerate the "insult and gave them a befitting reply".

The Gujarati business chambers were roped in. On February 21, 2003, some state-level business leaders floated

Resurgent Group of Gujarat and warned that any attempt to project unrealistic image of Gujarat outside the state will not be appreciated. This was the division within the industry I had experienced even during the peak of riots in early 2002.

Crucially for Modi, the group included Cadila Pharmaceuticals Chairman Indravadan Modi, Bakeri group Chairman Anil Bakeri, Nirma Ltd chairman Karsanbhai Patel, Ashima group Chairman Chintan Parikh and Executive Chairman of Nirma Education and Research Foundation NV Vasani.

Without naming the CII or its leaders, the group warned that "..... These forces need not misunderstand the peace-loving and tolerant attitude of Gujarat as its weakness", and maintained that the 'glory of Gujarat' could not be compromised.

Narendra Modi had played his card well again. He knew the pragmatic approach to Indian business was never to get isolated from a happening state like Gujarat. His state was neither a disturbed Kashmir or North East nor industry unfriendly states like Bihar or (then) Left-ruled West Bengal.

No Indian big and medium houses could think of carrying on with their business by ignoring Gujarat - which provided ample avenues both for business inputs and equally - if not more - rewarding outputs.

The CII leadership was pushed to the corner and ultimately peace was reportedly brokered by Arun Jaitley. In fact, falling short of an apology, CII in a letter taken to the Gujarat Chief Minister to his office by an office-bearer Tarun Das personally said: "we are sorry for the hurt and pain you have felt, and I regret very much the misunderstanding". And after the deal was done CII also facilitated the Gujarat government to organise an international meet in Zurich. Needless to add, those who know him closely, put it out aptly: that's Modi's signature style.

Politically, for Congress and his opponents within NDA and BJP, thus there is little to dispute that Modi makes a lethal combination of a Hindutva champion and an industry friendly development oriented leader. He and his admirers are rightly waiting for these to garner votes.

Chapter – 2

The Riots

Making of the Brand Modi

Till 27 February, 2002, Narendra Modi was another BJP leader and a Chief Minister. But his moment came when the Ahmedabad-bound Sabarmati Express from Faizabad was attacked by Muslims at Godhra station killing 58 *Kar Sevaks,* later to be described as *Ram Bhakts.*

He visited Godhra station and said his government viewed the attack on *Ram Bhakts,* who were returning from Ayodhya, seriously. His government termed the incident as 'pre-planned violent act of terrorism'. The Gujarat Minister of State for Home Gordhan Zadafia, then a trusted lieutenant of Modi and now a *bête noire,* said about forty people had been rounded up in connection with the attack on Sabarmati Express. He also volunteered to add that the incident could not be called communal violence "because there was no retaliation". In New Delhi, the Union Cabinet met for two hours in the night to take stock of the situation. The Prime Minister Atal Behari Vajpayee spoke to Chief Minister over phone and asked him to "firmly deal with the situation". The then Union Home Minister LK Advani also spoke to Modi. The Centre sounded a country-wide alert and directed the states to take suitable measures to maintain peace.

The gravity of the situation could be well understood as the Prime Minister linked Godhra incident to the vexed temple issue. Vajpayee asked the VHP to suspend its Ayodhya campaign of March 15, (2002) when it wanted to organise a *Shila Pujan*.

In the meantime, the charred bodies of the Godhra victims were brought to Ahmedabad. At Kalupur railway station in Ahmedabad, emotions ran high even as hours before at Godhra station when Modi inspected the charred compartment, reportedly an angry crowd including a few Bajrang Dal activists mobbed him. The message was getting clearer.

Giving their own signals about Hindu anger and possible retaliation, the VHP had called for a Bandh and issued a 24-hour deadline to the government to bring the culprits to book.

I was working with Press Trust of India (PTI) in Mumbai those days and was flown into Ahmedabad in an early morning flight on 28th February. In an unprecedented violence that followed, VHP observed Bandh to protest the incident.

Believing in eye for an eye theory, the Gujarat Hindus were looking for the opportune time to settle the "score against Muslims", as many activists later said. State machineries including police turned blind and VHP and Bajrang Dal activists virtually took charge of the streets in communally hyper sensitive Ahmedabad, state's commercial hub and the popular trader's paradise. Here came Modi's role as the Chief Minister and the need to do his duty in protecting the 'Raj Dharma' (ethics of governance). It is supposed to be these failures on the part of the Chief Minister that is being questioned even now.

Senior police officer Sanjiv Bhatt has accused the Chief Minister of complicity in the post-Godhra riots of 2002 and this has now snowballed into a major legal battle with the arrest of Bhatt and later his release after a fierce legal battle.

About eighty people, an overwhelming of them Muslims and mostly in Ahmedabad, were killed on the first day of insane rage.

In worst ever communal clash, Hindu men and women also took to the streets looting shops and renowned showrooms. Hotels and other business establishments owned by Muslims were ransacked and burnt. Twenty-six towns in the state were placed under curfew as arsonists took law into their hands with police mostly looking the other side. In somewhat a clear testimony of instructions from the very top – of course subject to be proved in a court of law – the police force had almost disappeared. Even traffic police personnel were not to be seen. Mass massacres took place in several places – two prominent of them being Gulberg Society in Chamanpura area and the minority-stronghold Naroda Patiya. Among others, former Congress MP Ehsan Jafri was charred to death by 2000-strong mob in Gulberg Society despite the politician reported to have called up police and "his politician friends" including the Chief Minister.

Jafri's wife Zakia had moved the Supreme Court and wanted Modi be charge-sheeted. The apex court has now said that everything related to the case must be settled in the trial court.

The Supreme Court has not ordered filing any chargesheet against the Chief Minister and this, we will see later, has been interpreted by Modi and the BJP as a certain relief for the beleaguered Chief Minister.

By evening of February 28, 2002, sitting in the PTI office at Hindu dominated Navrangpura Swastik Chowrasta, I had reports flooding in at my desk about destruction of Masjids including the popular Noorani Masjid, market place, residences of Muslims, Juhapura area and indiscriminate killings everywhere. In fact, the first day was only like a tip of iceberg as the arson and communal killings continued for weeks. Ahmedabad to me appeared a wilderness of pain and heartbreak.

It was difficult to confirm the casualty figures even from police control rooms as pressure was telling on the cops manning both the city control room at Shahibaugh and the state control room at Gandhinagar. Almost 27 towns and cities spread over 16 districts were placed under curfew. There was a steady stream of injured people including women and children coming to Ahmedabad's hospitals, mostly with burn injuries, stab injuries and sprinkles out of blasts of crude bombs. But surprisingly, no arrests were made in Ahmedabad on February 28, the first day of the post-Godhra retaliation.

The police officer in news these days Sanjiv Bhatt, then SP intelligence in Gandhinagar, had later told me that even on February 27 – that is one day ahead of VHP bandh, despite the Sangh Parivar's announcement of a true reaction to 'manifestation of Islamic fundamentalism', only eight people were taken into custody under preventive arrest. "The police authorities also did not work on all India suspect list vis-à-vis communal violence and did not take any mandatory action expected to be taken against communally bent of mind public figures like Ashok Bhatt and Pravin Togadia", he had said.

On February 28, as mass killings of Muslims were engineered allegedly by Hindu chauvinists in the name of seeking justice to Godhra killings, two senior ministers sat in police control rooms in Ahmedabad and Gandhinagar. The Gujarat Health Minister Ashok Bhatt, who also had certain charges against him, was provided access to police control room at commissioner's office at Shahibaugh in Ahmedabad, while Urban Development Minister and then the cabinet spokesman IK Jadeja, also a trusted lieutenant of Chief Minister Modi, had parked himself in state police control room at Gandhinagar for about four hours. The then Ahmedabad Police Commissioner PC Pandey later tried to make a defence of the entire episode saying the ministers were allowed access to the control rooms to 'facilitate' easy flow of government directions as Defence Minister George

Fernandes was also to visit Ahmedabad, the next day, on March 1, 2002.

It was for the first time, that any communal and ethnic conflict was marred by gross abuse of official position and documents - like voters' list and traders' licences. There was enough indication that a 'distinct pattern' of communal cleansing was carried out against Muslims, not sparing the women and children, especially in Ahmedabad and adjacent places.

However, in Ahmedabad even months after the riots, the local residents apparently showed approval for the violence and arson against the Muslims who were attacked irrespective of their economic status and profession.

Several hotels and eateries even with secular names like 'Kabir' and 'Millennium' were damaged. Even business establishments run by Muslims in partnership with Hindus were attacked. The message for Hindus in Ahmedabad and Gujarat who had befriended Muslims was perhaps clear - do not do business with 'meat eaters'.

"Loot was carried out driven by greed but there was an added refrain that they were looting the properties of the Muslims", lamented Rafiqa Bano of riot-hit Naroda Patiya - whose four children were killed and one daughter seriously injured in a blaze. There was also active participation of women from middle class Hindu families.

With such high rate of undiluted approval of anti-Muslim violence from the Hindus, the Chief Minister Modi could not actually take a different note - though as the custodian of the state's administration - he should have. Ten years and more after these, Modi does not like to field these questions.

In the meantime, my humble understanding is that such merciless killings and the loot could take place only on a soil 'fertile' with religious prejudices. Godhra and the post-Godhra ghosts would, therefore, haunt Gujarat and its people for a long time.

It is not without good reason that RSS veteran MG Vaidya, though unapologetic about the violence, told a news conference in Mumbai in August 2002, that the post-Godhra violence was "unlike a Hindu way of reaction". But these were the processes of creating the brand equity in Modi. Both the 2002 and 2007 assembly elections in Gujarat were treated as plebiscite on him and the BJP gamble paid. He is truly the poster boy of the party; though with a latent riddle.

Coming back to the 2002 incidents, the arsonists even razed the tomb of one of the best-known Urdu poets of the state Vali Gujarati. Many small shrines in the city were also destroyed during the frenzy that rocked Ahmedabad. At Shahibaugh at a stone's throw from city police commissioner's office, rioters demolished Vali Gujrati's tomb and a Hanuman shrine reportedly built over it promptly.

The anti-Muslim incidents had a 'salutary effect' in uniting the Hindus. Such unity in a caste-ridden Hindu society in Gujarat was no mean achievement for the believers of Hindutva. Modi was strongly regarded as someone who stood by the Hindus and thus in no time, he emerged a local hero and Sangh Parivar propagandists rightly called him 'Hindu *Hridaysamrat*'.

Thus, as police and administration went blind even as the VHP and Sanghi activists virtually took charge of the state, the Hindutva elements seemed quite emboldened by the backing they got. The confidence swelled into such height that the arsonists did not hesitate even to burn the offices of the Wakf Board and the Minority Finance Corporation located in the supposed-to-be 'high-security' Secretariat area in the state's seat of power and authority – Gandhinagar.

Brandishing swords and sticks, Bajrang Dal activists and other Hindu youths at many places screamed aloud that they were seeking justice and revenge for the 'well-planned' attack on *Ram Bhakts* in Godhra. Thousands of arsonists went on the rampage torching shops, Muslim colonies and public properties in both urban and rural areas across a number of districts. There was a clear refrain that they wanted to attack and loot only the Muslims. Mass killings were reported from Naroda Patiya and Meghaninagar. Gulberg Housing Society riots in Chamanpura area at least claimed 40 lives including former MP Jafri.

Not surprisingly, Modi based his entire thesis of communal violence on the Newton's much acclaimed time-tested Third Law of Motion. I have visited Ahmedabad and Gujarat more than once since 2002. Even on a brief visit prior to 2007 state assembly elections, I found there was hardly any change in the mindset of the Hindu population though the development bug of Modi had caught people's imagination well. Five years after 2002 insane killings and arson, one assessment was that during the initial hours of post-Godhra retaliation, Modi was not a direct accomplice to the violence; but he was rather caught almost clueless.

The polarization of Hindu voters suited him but the manner and the speed with which it came, even Modi was left surprised. According to some police and administrative reports, the Gujarat government thought the retaliation could go on maximum for 72 hours; that is three days. But it went for three months. "Modi had to justify the reaction of the majority voters. This endeared him to Hindus irrespective of caste factors", commented one retired state government employee during my interaction in November, 2007.

Modi could be singled out and even now there are groups and individuals within BJP who are singling him out for the 2002 holocaust. But I have throughout given the Gujarat Chief Minister the benefit of doubt. After all, he had replaced Keshubhai Patel, when BJP was at the receiving end of the electorate's anger. The BJP expected him to deliver Gujarat; and Modi did it like a true batting star of a limited over's game in a one-day cricket fashion – mustered the runs little bothering about playing unorthodox shots.

Speaking from Sangh Parivar point of view, the RSS-BJP-VHP triangular axis of the Sangh Parivar had succeeded in mobilizing unity of purpose within caste-ridden Hindus in Gujarat. This is no small achievement for the Parivar in Gujarat as according to a *Bombay Gazetteer*, Gujarat was pre-eminently a land of castes. "In 1827, there were as many as 207 castes in the city of Surat alone which did not marry outside their community", says *Gazetteer of Bombay Presidency* edited by British scholar James Campbell and published in 1901.

My findings following interactions with social analysts and academicians revealed that the Hindu mobilization was made possible due to the Ayodhya movement and it only gained momentum with each communal backlash since 1969, followed by 1985 and post-Babri Masjid demolition in 1992.

In many localities in 2002 during riot-torn days, even those from backward communities and dalits in Gujarat spoke the language and verb of Uma Bhartis, Ashok Singhals and Bal Thackerays.

It is significant to note that during the post-Godhra retaliation, the right wing Hindu leadership also won the support of Dalits and OBCs - especially the upwardly mobile strata in 1995 and 1998 assembly polls when BJP banked on slogans like '*Ram Mandir banana hai*' and '*Abki Bari Atal Behari*'.

The absence of third political force of caste-based leadership like Mayawati or Mulayam Singh Yadav was another factor that played a catalytic role in endearing the OBC and Dalit Hindus close to the Sangh Parivar and the BJP in Gujarat, rightly dubbed as the 'Hindutva laboratory'. Therefore, despite facing decades of negligence and deprivation from the upper castes, the backward castes joined ranks with majority Hindus and took to the streets in the name of Hindu revivalism. It is a vital aspect of the society in Gujarat which needs deeper studies that how despite ascendancy of caste identity consciousness and VP Singh's post-Mandal politics sweeping northern India, the communal polarization between Hindus and Muslims has survived and even grew sharper than of any conflict between different castes among the Hindus.

It is coincident that Modi has emerged a neo-champion of the Hindutva cause since 2002. In effect, all the hard work for Hindu polarization was led by the then Keshubhai Patel-led BJP government's tenure in tandem with influential VHP. The 'one Hindu' slogan of VHP was well- propagated by BJP. It had cemented the campaign of undivided identity of the Hindus despite the caste divisions. Local RSS office-bearers in Ahmedabad often refer to the former Chief Minister Keshubhai Patel's comment to a lower caste youth in Mehsana district during a RSS camp in 2001; "If you are a Harijan, I am a Harijan too. And if I am Patel, you are also Patel because we both are Hindus".

Interestingly, pragmatism of highly entrepreneur community, Vanias, has left other communities, including the Hindu backward castes, in the entire state, highly impressed.

Vanias form only 5-6 per cent of the population of the state. They are scattered throughout the state and thanks to their business acumen and economic success, their culture has virtually become 'synonymous' with Gujarati culture and perhaps also for those non-Gujaratis settled in Gujarat. The backward castes, bereft of any leader like Mayawati or Lalu Yadav, therefore, look forward to the trading class Vanias and to some extent to Rajputs and Brahmins, and automatically follow the religious or for that matter the communal lines of these communities. Thus, in the ultimate analysis we see that it is more than sheer coincidence that Modi has not only justified the Hindu anger and the subsequent violence in the state.

Days after senseless violence, mostly targeting the minority Muslims, the Gujarat Chief Minister was in no tune to express regrets for the killings. Though he had spoken about the five crore Gujaratis and their pride, he could not in effect convince the citizenry, especially Muslims, that he is truly the guardian of their lives and properties.

On one occasion, *Times of India* reported Modi's reaction to the insane rage quoting the Chief Minister as saying "every action has an equal and opposite reaction". The title of the page one story was aptly put: "Bad Physics". However, subsequently, at a press conference in Mumbai in last part of March, 2002, while killings still continued; Modi looked unfazed by the continued violence dismissing these as "*chhut phut ghatnaye* (merely ignorable incidents)". Importantly, he denied the Newton theory remark and said that as an art student he hardly understood what the statement really meant (sic). He also maintained that situation was normal or rather fast returning to normal. It is altogether a different matter that killings continued unabated for weeks even after his media meeting in Mumbai.

In the assembly polls on December 12, 2002, Modi emerged victorious with his brand name or Moditva. *Times of India*, in its editorial on December 16, a day after the counting of results, said, "five crore Gujaratis" as Modi kept describing, have given their stamp of approval for "Modi-ism".

Another leading news daily, *The Indian Express* echoed similar sentiments saying "the day (December 15, day of counting of votes) belonged to Narendra Modi who, riding the wave he whipped up after the Godhra attack, delivered Gujarat to the BJP and Sangh Parivar with a two-thirds majority".

Much to the satisfaction of BJP and its gamble on Modi-brand, the saffron party had romped home in Gujarat proving all the prophets of doom wrong. In fact, hardly any exit and opinion polls could predict such a landslide victory for Modi's BJP in December 2002 polls. In the 182-member assembly, BJP picked up as many as 127 seats.

Major poll pundits, magazines and newspapers had gone to the town saying that Congress under stewardship of Shankersinh Vaghela, a former RSS man, has managed to gain grounds. In a decisive mandate, which virtually ensured that Gujarat could be drenched in saffron, in Saurashtra region, where polarization was said to be minimal and Patels were said to be annoyed with the saffron party for dumping Keshubhai Patel, BJP maintained its dominance bagging 37 of 52 seats. It swept aside Congress in Rajkot district bagging nine out of 11 seats while making significant inroads into the traditional Congress bastion of central Gujarat. It picked up 41 out of 43 seats in the region. BJP also surged ahead in Northern region and tribal belts of Panchmahals and Dahod showing post-Godhra riots had sought to bring even tribals under the influence of Hindutva influence. The Modi brand had truly arrived in its full steam.

For next five years or for that matter the subsequent years till circa 2012, the story of Gujarat is synonymous with the story of its chief minister. Neither internal dissensions within the party nor any other issue has even for one day threatened Modi's undisputed position as the top most leader of Gujarat BJP.

Therefore, we also see that Modi-brand is essentially a qualitative Hindutva brand. No wonder, even at his *Sadbhavna* or goodwill fast in September 2011, there was no ventilation of remorse or apology from Modi for the 2002 riots. It's said and not without good reason that politicians do everything considering their electoral strategy. Going by this rationale, an apology could come from a *neta* only if there is a 'damaged relationship between a politician and his voters'.

In Modi's case, the relationship with his support base has not been damaged. Rather it has emerged a stronger bond since the riots as he is regarded largely as the only chief minister who stood by the majority Hindus, said to be waiting for justice for decades vis-à-vis the assertive politics of Muslims till 2002.

"For Brand Modi, it's the relationship with those who do not vote for him which is on the rocks and therefore, why should he really bother about it," explained one senior retired intelligence official, who served in Gujarat.

In other words, the 88 per cent Hindus are backing Modi to the hilt and it will perhaps only be a political hara-kiri if he tenders an apology for the 2002 misadventure in not acting against the alleged Hindu rioters. Thus, the 'Modi Brand' today cannot see beyond Hindutva plank and none other than Modi himself knows it pretty well.

"He is more an ear-to-the-ground politician. Look at the way Advani tried to come out of his Hindutva poster boy image by his remarks on secular Jinnah; he left his traditional Hindu vote base shaken and hardly benefited among Muslims," the intelligence official argued eloquently.

However, the *Sadbhavna* Fast launched in September 2011 and rather taken into rural areas of Gujarat was definitely aimed towards 're-branding of Modi'. But it was not directed to turn 'secular' overnight as Advani's misadventure was a lesson for Modi too. Instead, Modi now wants to project his brand equity as a 'developmental mode'. How much of that would affect the voters' mind, however remains to be seen.

Modi's determination to stay put his core constituency; the hardliner Hindutva is somewhat able to make the impact as his political honesty. So much is his acceptability even among non-resident Indians that in 2007 after the assembly polls, Shreyas Suresh, wrote in his blog from Chicago: "Recent Indian political history has seen a decline of strong and honest leaders. Mr Modi is one of the last remaining few. People might call him an authoritarian, but the need of the moment is just that. He has not only turned Gujarat into a model state with terrific development but also given the people a corruption free government".

All these years Modi has been very tactful too. He is constantly playing as someone dealing with an uncooperative Central Government headed by Congress-led coalition. So his repeated attempts are to play the central ill-treatment meted to non-Congress states.

However, his attempt to become an anchor of the anti-Congress politics is not making much headway as JD (U) leader Nitish Kumar continues to play spoilsport and his own mentor, LK Advani in pursuance of his *Rath Yatra* against corruption has only tried to put himself in the race for the hot seat.

We have seen earlier in this book, how the differences between Advani and Modi are now getting reflected more. In May 2012, as I come to last stages of going through the manuscript once again, perhaps LK Advani's days in BJP vis-à-vis a major role politically are dwindling. Thus, the slot could easily go to Narendra Modi at least within BJP and notwithstanding the objections from NDA partners. To them also, Modi camp would be telling candidly, stay with us and see whether we (Modi brand equity) can bring votes. This is what counts in a democracy.

Nursing the clear ambition to become the BJP's prime ministerial candidate in 2014, Modi thus ought to reinvent himself to gain wider acceptability. It is perhaps with this issue in mind that his poster was put in Ahmedabad airport, albeit for the first time, to wish good luck to the Haj pilgrims. Clearly determined to ensure that the minority community does not upset his electoral prospects, both in 2012 assembly polls and 2014 Lok Sabha polls; for the first time, Modi and several other BJP leaders have reached out to Haj pilgrims. In October 2011, huge hoardings showing saffron leaders wishing pilgrims "Haj Mubarak" were displayed at the Ahmedabad airport. Modi's poster showed not only the Chief Minister waving at the pilgrims but also requested them to pray for Gujarat's development. In the past, only Haj Committee members were seen on the posters.

At one end, Modi's hypnotic oratorical skill and theatrical flair – for instance the 'Mia Musharraf' rhetoric and '*hum panch hamare pachis*' – are forcing critics to compare him with Hitler and a 'Muslim-hater'. Few others find in him glimpses of Singapore's Lee Kuan Yew, who once famously spoke about the need for trade between democracy and discipline. For Modi, it's a right balance of hardliner Hindu chauvinism and development. In the ultimate though, it's the ***Moditva*** – that remains his lasting legacy.

However, it ought to be stated that Modi needs to be careful in pursuing his ambitions for a nationwide acceptability and ultimately to be crowned as BJP's or for that matter NDA's candidate for the prized office of prime minister. Perhaps his detractors think Modi could go the Kalyan Singh way if he is overestimating his own strengths. Like former UP chief minister, Modi is also no Vajpayee.

Even the party stalwart and the original Hindutva mascot LK Advani had to struggle hard to retain his position as the leader of the party after his Jinnah-remark hara-kiri. As a matter of fact, Advani also stood isolated after 2005 Jinnah-secular misadventure and he had to ultimately give up BJP presidentship and after 2009 poll debacle, the Leader of the Opposition post. In fact, even others like Balraj Madhok had to bite the dust once he was shown the doors by the Sangh Parivar fountainhead, the RSS.

But those who know Modi maintain that he knows the size of his *'chadar'* (read shoes). Anyone different from Modi's personality would have found it extremely difficult to survive the manner he has managed the tight-rope walking. This native sense of understanding the ground politics, undoubtedly, keeps him going.

Years back, former Nagaland chief minister who also served as Himachal Pradesh Governor, Hokishe Sema, known as the protagonist of nationalism among the few pro-India Naga leaders, had said that the Indian political system over the years generally prescribed for status quo. An atmosphere would always be created wherein individual aspirations and 'out-of-the-box' thinking would be strongly resisted.

After making a closer scrutiny of Gujarat politics and Modi's approach to it, I am tempted here to maintain that Modi's politics perhaps brings that different genre.

Going back to Naga leader Hokishe Sema's diagnosis of the Indian polity; it is a fact that to survive and thrive in a political atmosphere that Modi inherited especially after post-2002 riots and highly successful election, one needs to have some peculiar qualities.

Modi has in him that combined magic box of native understanding, trust in some hardliner ideology, willingness to manipulate things and an astute sense of humour and importantly the timing.

The theatrical perfection - of 'Mia Musharraf' rhetoric and '*hum panch hamare pachis*' lines have added to his public image rather than harming him despite the large scale criticism.

One likes it or not; knowing very well that he is a loner in the game - and more so if he is on the top - Modi is creditably displaying personal commitment to achieve the excellence in his career.

His officials admire him for his gruelling attention to details - when he ensures getting complete information about an issue or a person he has to confront; on the other hand, he is a tested hand in macro-management also. The strong sense of self-confidence has also made him ruthless, like the manner he denied the ticket to the late Haren Pandya for 2002 assembly elections braving the entire party leadership including Atal Behari Vajpayee. Yet again, in 2011, he was uneasy with party president Nitin Gadkari reinstating his *bête noire* Sanjay Joshi. He also displayed the tenacity in handling Pravin Togadia and the clinical precision he applied to sideline the one-time vocal VHP leader.

Thus, when Keshubhai Patel and others lament today in circa 2012 about Narendra Modi going dictator, it is not the first time.

Modi's best time is perhaps yet to come. But Modi does a good balance between his strengths and the possible areas of problems he could face while dealing with some issues.

For instance, he did not hesitate to take the first step in clearing the ambiguity over his supposed differences with LK Advani. On November 7, 2011, a day after former deputy prime minister's 6th *Rath yatra* entered Gujarat, Modi sought to clarify that there was no difference between him and his mentor Advani.

He was reacting to reports that there were cold vibes between him and Advani and even there was a vacant chair (spot) between the two the previous day on the dais. "It is all a handiwork of the media barons", Modi said in the presence of Advani, whom he accompanied in the specially-configured bus for two days to drive home the point that all was well between the two Hindutva mascots. Modi had said that the chair "remained vacant because state party president RC Faldu was delivering his speech".

In the subsequent period came Modi's high-profile China visit. Diplomatically, it is an historic role played by Beijing in snubbing the US and also giving the 'first credible' international forum to Modi. "The success of Gujarat has today put it in a place where it can negotiate and navigate international relations of direct economic consequence to it without being held back by the timidity in New Delhi", wrote Shashi Shekhar in website rediff.com.

On January 27, 2012, the newsletter from Swarnim Gujarat claimed that in a survey spread across 19 states, as many as 24 per cent of respondents had favoured Modi as the prime minister as against the 17 per cent of his closest competitor Rahul Gandhi. It maintained that Modi's standing has improved from nine per cent in August 2010 and 12 per cent in January 2011.

Under him even the worst of critics have to agree that the state of Gujarat is growing faster than any state. "......10 years on (since the carnage) whilst the controversy is still being debated, it isn't stopping business from flowing in (Gujarat)", said BBC in its report on the eve of the completion of 10 years of the country's worst religious violence.

In terms of his re-branding vis-à-vis as a 'development chief minister'; observers feel the single most right thing happening in Gujarat under Modi is that the business and industry are treated with priority. There is no lip-service or politics of shifting a matter by passing the buck to certain excuses or as they say, bureaucratic bottlenecks. Instead, all commitments made by Modi have been served to the industry. At least the entire apparatus seemed to be busy delivering the goods.

The 'Modi brand' has paradoxically caught the Congress in quite a quagmire-like situation. In January 2012, Sonia Gandhi's outfit launched a satire-advertisement but the same proved counter-productive. The advertisement had listed the achievements of all the chief ministers in Gujarat since 1960 to prove the point that Modi was 'not the sole claimant of all the credits', as reported in *The Hindu*.

Though the Congress leaders said the advertisement was 'a satire' but the message ended up saying that "the Chief Minister Modi was a master organiser and astute election strategist". The Congress managers maintained that the party only intended to 'mock' at Modi's towering and most of the time highly misleading campaign that: even Narmada dam came during his time – to which Congress counter-argument has been that nearly 110 metres of the dam construction was completed before Modi came at the helm of affairs.

The Gujarat Congress spokesman merely had said: "What we are trying to convey through the advertisement is that the Gujarat's progress is not due to one person (that is Modi)".

But to take the debate on acceptability of Modi as the prime ministerial candidate of BJP-led NDA coalition, it can be stated that the chances only seems remote. On January 24-25, 2012 the Janata Dal (United) of Nitish Kumar hinted strongly that by 2014 it would like to project the Bihar Chief Minister for the country's top most political post.

In a totally non-political event, the birth anniversary of former chief minister and veteran socialist Karpoori Thakur, at Patna, the Janata Dal leaders including the ministers in Nitish cabinet literally urged their chief minister to take over the reins of the nation.

The Bihar unit JD(U) chief Vashishtha Narayan Singh made it amply clear about the party's agenda placing Nitish

Kumar in direct competition with the incumbent Prime Minister Dr Manmohan Singh. "Two types of economies are in competition in India – one is economics of Manmohan Singh favouring the multi-national companies and the other is economics of Nitish Kumar which is based on development with justice".

Bihar minister for Scheduled Castes and Scheduled Tribes welfare Jitan Ram Manjhi was also equally candid: "Time has come for Nitish Kumar to seriously consider about leading the country".

Modi's worries are, thus, far beyond Gadkaris, Sanjay Joshis or even the veteran LK Advani. However posters in Gujarat related to dispute between Joshi and Modi, have adversely effected the party's image.

Chapter – 3

Hindutva Laboratory

Unique combination of geography and history has made Gujarat a fertile ground for Hindutva. Gujarat's geographical location in close proximity to Maharashtra, which witnessed initial days of the Hindu fundamentalism upheaval after RSS was founded in 1925, is also a factor that contributed towards polarized situation.

The organizations like RSS though were founded in Maharashtra, but the network immediately spread to Gujarat with Marathi Brahmins taking up the '*Shakha Pramukh*' roles while native Gujaratis generally confined themselves to the business. There was also absence of influence of any major reform movement in Gujarat in the late 18th and 19th centuries. This has resulted in Hinduism to be understood in a slightly different paradigm. This school prescribes adopting a monolithic policy for survival. Those who propound this brand of Hinduism, slightly differ with the essential accommodating and compassionate features of *Sanatan Dharma* (Hinduism) and are generally blinded by their hatred towards the expansion of Islam and also Christianity.

Gujarat's location along the international borders and sea coast exposed the state to repeated Muslim invasions, something that would not be perhaps understood in other parts of India. Local historians point out how the natives have over the generations cultivated hatred towards Muslim invaders, especially the Turco-Persian ruler Mahmud Ghazni, who had destroyed the seaside Hindu temple of Somnath in 1025.

The torment of destruction of Somnath temple had remained over the decades. Even Sardar Patel and Pt Jawaharlal Nehru had allowed reconstruction of the same, whereas BJP stalwart LK Advani's Ram *Rath Yatra*, which created an awesome tidal wave of Hindu nationalism, had started from Somnath on 25th September, 1990.

In Gujarat, Sangh Parivar outfits, like RSS and VHP did all in their capacity to use their chauvinism tool to keep the flame of religious polarization burning.

These organizations really provided to the aggrieved section of Hindus "a true Hindu voice lost by shameless Muslim appeasement" to create vote bank by the Congress. It's on this backdrop that during one of his trips to Ahmedabad, Ashok Singhal of VHP had said, "the Hindu unity you are talking was long overdue. We ought to come together as Hindus and be proud of it".

In January 2003, Modi endorsed this argument rather strongly. At his first rally outside Gujarat after the 2002 assembly elections, on 12th January, 2003 rally at Shivaji Park at Dadar, Mumbai, he urged the people "not to be shy or apologetic about Hindutva".

Therefore, it is not without good reason that Modi has not expressed any regret for the 2002 incidents, nor did he oblige the Muslim cleric when he rejected the request to put on a Muslim skull cap.

His camp is blatant in defending Chief Minister's decision not to regret about the anti-Muslim riots. "How can a Chief Minister say sorry, when his voters in overwhelming manner do not feel sorry about 2002 riots," remarked a BJP MP, who also attended Modi's *Sadbhavna* Fast in September 2011.

It will not be out of place to mention here that such Hindutva polarization has come to stay even outside Gujarat. The constant appeasement of Muslims by Congress, Left and other secular brigade and the deprivation of jobs for upper caste Hindus due to reservation policies often on faulty yardsticks have angered the upper middle class of Hindu society. Therefore, a large section of Hindus see that there is a good reason to be assertive about own rights.

This is not merely confined to Gujarat as I know of several youths from Mumbai to North East echoing these sentiments. These sections see post-Godhra retaliation as only a manifestation to settle age-old injustice and exploitation of the Hindus.

The Hindus strongly feel the hurt of continuous raids and destruction of their temples by Muslim rulers. The holy city of Mathura, the birthplace of Lord Krishna, became a prime target from the 10th and 11th century onwards. Mahmud of Ghazni raided Mathura in 1017. In subsequent period, almost entire north India came under Muslim domination with the invaders establishing their capital in Agra, not very far from Mathura.

Varanasi, anglicized Benaras, and known to Hindus as 'Kashi' was another major Hindu hub which became target of Muslim tirade. It was a famous pilgrim centre for Hindus for conducting last rites and other pious activities besides a centre of learning. But a century old golden period for Varanasi came to an end abruptly by Muslim invasions. The Muslim military commander Qutub-ud-din Aibak ransacked and looted Varanasi in 1194 destroying hundreds of temples and building mosques. In the 14th century, by 1375-76, Firoz Shah also ordered destruction of Hindu temples. In 1496, under Sikander Lodi there was yet another series of destructions and the city was even renamed Mohammadabad. The period under Akbar encouraged mutual tolerance and even two popular temples came up in Varanasi. But the period under Aurangzeb again brought in demolitions of temples. In 1659, one popular Krittivasesvera temple was destroyed and allegedly a mosque constructed in its place. Aurangzeb tried the same phenomenon in 1669 with yet another major temple.

In the 19th century, under the colonial masters, even Christian missionaries tried to establish their toehold but largely the city had braved through the challenges to remain a Hindu stronghold even up to this day.

Therefore, in the streets of Ahmedabad or gullies of Rajkot, even years after the carnage, one could hardly see a sense of '*afsos* (regrets)' among the common Hindu population, both Gujaratis and non-Gujaratis. In 2002, super cop KPS Gill, who became Chief Minister's Security Advisor for a short period, had also diagnosed that Kalinga phenomenon was absent in the state. In normal circumstances, the 'remorse' or the feeling of guilt for such large-scale violence should have dawned among the Hindus. This did not. Truly, here is a 'fertile' soil with religious prejudices and a test case to experiment religious fundamentalism, the Hindutva laboratory, as they put it.

Among the Hindu organizations in Gujarat, one could find that VHP and Bajrang Dal truly, are able to touch the pulse of Hindus, apparently the new generation of hardliners. It only stood endorsed during *Sadbhavna* Fast of Modi when he said, "my government has not done anything for minority or even for majority. Whatever the Gujarat government does, we do it for all". The reaction was expectedly a roaring applause. This only shows the shrewd politician in Modi. He could eye beyond his pocket-burrow state of Gujarat and look for wider acceptability natiowide, but he is well sticking to BJP's core values: no appeasement for Muslims or others. This keeps him on the winning side especially with the younger generation both in Gujarat and outside Gujarat.

Even in cosmopolitan Delhi, several journalists seemed to have enjoyed the remarks that a government should not do anything extra for any community. It must be equal to law when the law of the land is supposedly equal.

Here I would like to reflect upon a list of questionnaire circulated by the Gujarat unit of VHP addressed to "pseudo-secularists', who came running to Gujarat" during 2002. The one and half page document, signed by the general secretary, Dilipbhai Trivedi, had charged the leaders of "all hue and colour, aged, old or young, busy or free, all in their fineries whether Jodhpuri suits or spotless white khadis, who descended upon Gujarat with the sole purpose of getting free publicity and to malign Hindu name". Questions posed in the VHP's pamphlet were apparently those which common Hindus have asked and have not been really answered by 'secularists'.

Some of them were:

- Why did not these secular leaders visit Gujarat's Godhra the day of the burning alive of the Hindus in Godhra?
- By descending upon Gujarat and by visiting Muslim minority area only, did not these leaders insult the memories of those brutally burnt alive in Godhra?
- Why the unsolicited rush to Gujarat? But did they ever think of such visits over killing of hundreds of innocent Amarnath Yatris, who were being put under the Muslim sword?

In 2002, after the crucial assembly polls on the backdrop of anti-Muslim incidents, what came to light by quite a convincing statement was that Congress, once the dominant political party, was reduced to a passive force. During the three-month long riots, the Congress leaders could not come forward, as expected of them to protect Muslims.

There were reports that Congressmen were not to be seen despite frantic phone calls from the Muslims. Instead, the Congress leaders merely sat on dharna at Gandhi Ashram. They even paraded leaders from other states provoking no fear among arsonists but only ridicule from rival politicians.

It was only a test case of 'soft secularism' and a sort of Hindu appeasement that Sonia Gandhi appointed a former RSS man Shankersinh Vaghela as the Pradesh Congress chief. In course of my interactions with minorities, it was also revealed that they were looking forward towards emergence of a third political alternative.

In December 2002, immediately after the assembly poll results were declared, Congress leader Shankersinh Vaghela, one time associate of Modi and a former RSS pracharak, attributed the defeat to the 'misuse of Hindutva'. Little did he recall that even his party was not quite playing the genuine secularism card in Gujarat. One primary factor for the overwhelming Modi wave is the Congress refusal to offer itself as a viable secular force. In short, Vaghela had brought in only 'soft Hindutva' or 'vanilla secularism' as described by Shekhar Gupta of *The Indian Express*.

In fact, so much has been the pressure and influence among the electorate in Gujarat about the Hindu chauvinism agenda that on both the occasions, 2002 and 2011, in Congress virtually gave up all its talks about anti-RSS and Sangh Parivar's communal agenda when it turned its option on the former RSS functionary Shankersinh Vaghela as Congress party's chief player to take on Modi. Congress is trying out the same Vaghela card for 2012 battle royal too.

It is not without good reason that Modi had rightly taunted Sonia Gandhi in 2002 by saying, "I thank Jesus Christ that he had given the right sensibility to her to appoint a former RSS man as Congress chief in Gujarat".

The success of BJP and Modi in 2007 was perhaps a clearer message that if in 2002 they had won riding on the wave of Hindu polarization, in 2007 the credit for yet another landslide victory ought to be given to Modi and his brand of politics, 'the Moditva', as they put it.

Finally, the BJP tally of 117 seats, a modest drop of only 10 seats as against 127 of 2002 and the lead of 11 percentages over the Congress proved that in ground politics, things have hardly changed in Gujarat. This was the result even after 2004 electoral debacle suffered by BJP in Lok Sabha polls – and mostly attributed to BJP's mishandling of Gujarat 2002.

In contrast, in 2007 polls, Moditva was in play. But, political observers say Moditva could not be simply dismissed as another variety of Hindu communalism though it is definitely an offshoot of that radical politics. Moditva in effect, according to a former DGP of Gujarat, was taken to a new plane – meaning good packaging of Gujarati (pride) nationalism in a Hindutva frame and also including in it the master-card of development. By December 2007, Gujarat's growth was about 12 per cent and the master-card by Modi was not only that people spoke about the developments, the Gujarat poll managers for BJP under the joint stewardship of Narendra Modi and Arun Jaitley ensured that the much sullied Chief Minister (for secularism) gets the entire credit for the growth graph. "This was, however, not easy as by 2001 Gujarat was quake-hit and communally unsafe place", remarks the former police officer.

Now, heading towards 2012 assembly polls, Modi wants to repeat for the saffron party what Indira Gandhi could do to Congress once in 1970s when the brand Indira was a "plus factor" appealing to the voters often bypassing the Congress party structure and vote base.

BJP watchers say, this is something Atal Behari Vajpayee had reaped in 1996 and 1998 but had paradoxically failed to galvanize the votes for the 2004 parliamentary polls. In urban India, Manmohan Singh was the beneficiary of the same yardstick in 2009 Lok Sabha polls. The middle class Indians were convinced that Manmohan Singh's nuclear deal with the United States was in country's interest and those who opposed it – from the Left to Mayawati and Ajit Singh to Advani-led BJP - were entirely indulging in knee-jerk anti-Americanism.

But a crucial limitation of this image-game for 'Moditva' is that due to certain peculiarity of Indian socio-political scenario, the 'package' could not reap as much benefit outside Gujarat as it did in Gujarat. Even in the so-called BJP stronghold states, this card has a limited utility factor. In 2003, the Modi phenomenon failed in Himachal Pradesh, something admitted by Vajpayee himself.

One need not go too far. In 2010, JD(U)-BJP combine made a sweep at the Bihar polls even as Narendra Modi was completely kept out of the state.

Even in 2012 Uttar Pradesh polls; it was a tactical move by the BJP leadership when they kept Modi out of election campaign fearing polarization of Muslim votes in favour of the Congress.

But in the run up to the 2012 assembly polls, Congress has fallen back on former RSS pracharak Vaghela, they think who can take on Modi. This decision has come despite Vaghela suffering a loss of his parliamentary seat from Panchmahal in 2009 elections. Moreover, the Gujarat Congress is also afflicted with fierce battle among its rank and file. It goes without saying that making Vaghela the chairman of campaign committee has not gone down well in party circles. It is on the backdrop of this reason that on September 5, 2011, a rare joint press conference was addressed by leader of the opposition in the assembly Shaktisinh Gohil, Gujarat unit party president Arjun Modhwadia and Shankersinh Vaghela.

"There are no differences between us. We will work together till the assembly elections of 2012", Gohil volunteered to clarify and added that the party will 'benefit' from Vaghela's experience.

It ought to be mentioned here that Vaghela as a politician is altogether a fish of different pond. His one-time compatriots in the BJP and now detractors say the self-seeking inconsistence stance is the hallmark of his political approach. "We are glad the Congress has started mishandling their very electoral policy in Gujarat yet again. Vaghela as their general offers a unique advantage to us," said a key member of Gujarat cabinet. The sarcasm is not without good reason as even Gordhan Zadafia of fledgling Maha Gujarat Janata Party echoes similar sentiments. Actually, Vaghela has to blame himself for these backhanded remarks he is often described with.

Even prior to be named as in-charge of Congress election campaign committee, Vaghela was toying with the idea of joining Sharad Pawar-led NCP. Only on 8th August, 2011, Gujarat NCP chief, Jayant Bosky told media in Ahmedabad that Vaghela was already camping in Delhi for talks with NCP chief Sharad Pawar and Praful Patel for joining the NCP. But by September 5, less than a month, he took upon himself the mantle to lead the Congress campaign yet again.

Belonging to Kshatriya (Rajput) caste, Vaghela is also fondly called 'Bapu'. He has served Gujarat as the chief minister after he rebelled against BJP and floated a party of his own. A former chief minister from 1996 to 1997, he lost the Panchmahal Lok Sabha seat to Prabhansinh Chouhan of BJP in 2009. He was union textile minister in the Manmohan Singh government in UPA-I from 2004 to 2009.

Even the likes of Gohil, reportedly unhappy for the Congress high command decision think that Vaghela has already crossed his prime in Gujarat politics. Immediately after his appointment as the in-charge of party's campaign panel, Vaghela tried to fight his old foe Narendra Modi in his own game.

Probably at the cost of embarrassing party's national spokespersons who had dubbed Modi's three-day *Sadbhavna* Fast as 'gimmick', Vaghela announced a 'counter fast' at Gandhi Ashram in Ahmedabad beginning on September 17, 2011, the day Modi launched his fast.

In the run up to the 2002 polls, I had once asked Vaghela whether as a Congressman he would criticise RSS for the riots and also 'disown' the 'communal organisation'. Vaghela would merely say, "Why are you raising an old issue?" Here was the Congress chief warrior refusing to even speak against RSS.

Readers would find it interesting to note that Vaghela had also fielded a group of religious leaders led by the popular Bapu Murari to pitch in for the party, but the gamble never worked.

The Congress should have got a message vis-à-vis utility factor of Vaghela even during his counter-fast in Ahmedabad. "It was a slap in the face for Shankersinh Vaghela to discover his Kshatriya clansmen in the rival (Modi) camp", wrote Coomi Kapoor in *The Indian Express* referring to a host of Gujarat's princely families and their icons landing at the fast venue of Narendra Modi. "Many remarked on the large presence of Muslims at Narendra Modi's *Sadbhavna* Fast, but few noticed that the Gujarat Chief Minister scored another coup in successfully wooing the former princes and kings of Saurashtra, who have been diehard supporters of the Congress since 1960. Modi has been quietly working on Gujarat's princely families by helping to settle long-pending land disputes", she wrote.

Thus, at least on the face value, Gujarat was not merely a Hindu laboratory for Modi, his popularity and acceptability practically creates a situation that there are no challengers to him. I would, however, like to emphasize eloquently that between Congress and BJP, as well as among other political parties, like the Communists, nobody has the right to plead ignorance and adopt holier than thou approach on their respective contributions in vitiating the atmosphere in Gujarat and elsewhere in the country.

Today we know Modi symbolizes transformation of Gujarat with his development card.

But it's a fact; he has transformed the state the manner not quite expected under normal circumstances. He has brought in development and economic prosperity with a claim on better accountability of the government/ bureaucracy, but apparently there is a gamble in it. The state is today found positioning solely on its defence as well as hatred against Muslims. Much of these anti-Muslim trends are unjustified, uncalled for. The similar anti-Modi rhetoric of his detractors and secular brigade only indicate towards a more dangerous trend. Gujarat does need 'reconciliation' that brings an end to the 'demonisation' of the battered minority community on one side and the state chief minister on the other. His *Sadbhavna* Fast starting from Gandhinagar in September 2011 and later taken to hinterland lost its purpose and went off track due to political hyperboles as it was more linked to Modi's prime ministerial ambitions. But there is need of a neo-Hindutva culture in the one time laboratory of Hindutva, that would emphasize on tolerating the voice of dissent, accommodating minorities and show respect to the institutions, places of worship of different communities and upholding the rule of law.

The other side too needs to give up the prism of hatred towards the state's chief minister. The social activists and secular brigade including the Congress should appreciate the kind of ground reality in Gujarat and instead try offer a viable secular and credible alternative. Moditva cannot be replaced by 'soft secularism' of Congress. The people of Gujarat have rejected this attempt in the past and probably would do it again. They would accept Modi's hardliner chauvinism along with the tested development than the opportunism of soft secularism.

Chapter – 4

Development of Gujarat under Modi

On 7th October, 2011, the Narendra Modi government completed eleven years in office. A little more than four years ago, on 1st June, 2007, Narendra Modi became the longest serving Chief Minister of Gujarat. Prior to that in 2002, following the loss of two assembly seats in by-elections, BJP satrap in Gujarat Keshubhai Patel had to resign yielding power to Narendra Modi.

In 2002 December assembly elections, Modi won a landslide victory bagging 126 out of 182 seats riding a strong Hindutva wave generated by post-Godhra incidents. Then, there was no talk of development as Gujarat had rightly emerged as a laboratory for the most militant variety of right-wing Hindu nationalism in the history of independent India. Within a month since the historic victory in the heat and dust of Gujarat polity, Maharashtra BJP stalwart Gopinath Munde announced at a rally at Shivaji Park, Dadar in Mumbai in the presence of Modi that his party was eager to repeat the Gujarat formula of Hindutva in the state.

Five years later, on 23 December, 2007, the BJP and Modi yet again won the state elections in Gujarat and Narendra Modi became the Chief Minister for the third time in a row.

With BJP already out of office in Delhi since 2004, the Congress had hoped to turn the tide in Gujarat too. But the landslide victory in 2007 with Modi's party picking up 117 seats predictably sparked off the debate whether Modi won because of his charisma, because of his Hindutva image or economic development of the state since 2001.

Subjected to too much criticism for 2002 mishandling of riots in 2007, Modi just could not repeat the Hindutva card once more. Moreover, the ignominy of 2005 when the US had declined him Visa was still fresh in public memories as well as in the memory of a shrewd politician Modi.

He could not depend solely on Hindutva discourse and therefore, he shrewdly packaged Hindutva image with the development card.

Contrast to this in 2002, immediately after the results, Congress general to the Gujarat battle, Shankersinh Vaghela, attributed BJP's victory to "misuse of Hindutva" even as he sought to caution the voters against Modi government's failure in providing jobs and water. "Victory may come and victory may go. But even Hindus would need water and electricity", he had said.

Thus, governance was in the air in 2007 amid the heat and dust of Gujarat politics. But Modi was playing his cards well, often close to his chest. He knew the best bet for him in 2007 polls would be a good synthesis between hardliner Hindu leader and a pro-development Chief Minister.

Therefore, along with dishing out cold statistics of improvement in Gujarat situation since 2001, when it was drought prone and in 2002, a communally polarized state, the Chief Minister aptly highlighted the Ram Setu issue, and time and again highlighted 'terrorism' – a byword for Muslims. But as analysed later by an intelligence official in Delhi, "The Hindutva image and a match winner in Modi soon overshadowed the campaign after Sonia Gandhi made *maut ka saudagar* (merchant of death) remark and Modi eloquently justified the cold-blooded encounter killing of Sohrabuddin Shaikh.

At an election rally in Jamnagar district on December 4, 2007, Modi admitted that encounter killing of Sohrabuddin, a small time criminal, "happened in Gujarat, and if Sonia Gandhi wants she can hang me for this". The mandate, subsequently, is the part of the rest of the history. The BJP leaders later maintained that infusion of Sohrabuddin episode in the mid-way during the campaign helped BJP consolidate its vote base as this streamlined coming together of Modi's strong points: terrorism, pride of Gujarat, Congress appeasement of Muslims and of course the Hindutva belief on the righteousness of Hindus and the 'sin' of being Muslims.

It was only after these polls; Modi dedicated himself solely to the goal of changing his image to a pro-development man. In circa 2011, Gujarat managed a turnaround and achieved 11 per cent agricultural growth, according to state government officials despite its fast track industrial development. His opponents attribute the success to the state of Gujarat and the people of Gujarat's 'process of survival and high talent for entrepreneurship'. But the march towards progress in the field of agriculture, infrastructural facilities like drinking water, education, employment, transportation, manufacturing and tourism is certainly heartening.

"Ten years ago, Gujarat farmers' agriculture income was Rs 14,000 crore that has risen to Rs 80,000 crore today. The average agricultural growth rate of the country is less than three per cent while Gujarat's has crossed the double digit figure of nearly eleven per cent. He (the farmer) is using drip irrigation, green house, net house and sprinkler techniques to maximize profit with minimum investment. Due to soil health card, the productivity of the land has multiplied giving new directions to the agriculture sector", the Chief Minister said in an interview in October 2011.

Observers maintain that Narendra Modi's administration has pursued 'strategic planning' to bring about agricultural and industrial growth parallel to each other even as it addressed social sector issues too.

Seeking to clarify that Modi's brand of developments under the banner of vibrant Gujarat, were not basically for big industries often neglecting the social sector, in 2011 at the vibrant Gujarat summit, they say the state government deliberately focused on the financial uplift of rural poor to make them self-sufficient through a programme called Mission Mangalam.

"In Mission Mangalam, not only the state government but reputed corporate houses will also make joint-efforts. The strength of Gujarat lies in its 50 per cent population comprising of women. If women are included in the path of progress then the pace of development will be faster and widespread. I am committed to adding the strength of Nari Shakti as partners to development and decision-making. For this I wished to extend economic activity support to women and created *sakhi mandals* throughout Gujarat. Mission Mangalam is one such enterprise that helps the poorest of the poor women. Whether it is celebrating marriage or tending to sickness of her son or daughter, she need not depend on any external help. Lakhs of *sakhi mandals* have been integrated with banks leaving the management of over Rs 1000 crore in their hands. It is our desire to take this amount to Rs 5,000 crore. Just imagine if this huge amount is managed by poor women, how much progress they would have really achieved", the Chief Minister said in an interview circulated through his publicity newsletter.

On the Vibrant Summit neglecting the small and medium industries, the Chief Minister says such a notion is only based on "a big misconception". The country's five per cent population lives in Gujarat which has six per cent of the country's land mass and its GDP share is ten per cent. In this the contribution of nearly four lakh small and medium industries from Gujarat cannot be ignored.

The country's 70 per cent salt production is in Gujarat and the state also leads in caustic soda production (90 per cent); chemicals (60 per cent); petrochemicals (50 per cent); pharma (40 per cent); and polished diamonds (80 per cent). Business in salt, pharma and chemicals is largely run by small scale entrepreneurs and is a large contributor to national growth. This has brought in multi-faceted developments. On one hand, Gujarat is an emerging auto hub of India while on the other it has also become the textile and petro capital.

Under Modi's stewardship and a true CEO-like approach; Gujarat organized five Vibrant Summits in the last decade and placed the state on the world map. In the summit of 2011 alone, 7,936 MoUs were signed with investment commitment of Rs 20.83 lakh crore. This staggeringly high investment also promised to create over 52 lakh local jobs. In agro based industries, MoUs worth Rs 81,600 crore have been signed.

Creditably for his efforts, Narendra Modi has been the Chief Minister of Gujarat since 2001, leading Gujarat's population to unprecedented changes in wealth, infrastructure and social development. Officials say Gujarat's reforms are internationally recognised and have won the United Nations Public Service Award for improving transparency, accountability and responsiveness.

The Canadian Bombardier Transportation, which is churning out compartments for high-speed intra-city transportation has set up its unit at Savli near Vadodara at an estimated expenditure of $ 41 million and will provide the compartments to Delhi Metro and similar ventures in other cities as well as serve as a hub for exporting to South East Asia.

The easy accessibility of ports is truly vital. Gujarat already has 40 ports that handle 80 per cent of India's traffic and 20 per cent of its cargo. The state is promoting at least four private ports - Mundra, Pipapav, Kandla and Dholera.

Adequate power availability is another crucial asset. It is a power-surplus state both in coal-based thermal power and solar energy usage. The Asian Development Bank has approved a $100 m loan to Gujarat to build a 500 megawatt solar park.

Fortunately for Gujarat, the state is the biggest benefactor in the proposed Delhi-Mumbai Industrial Corridor as nearly 35-40 per cent of this corridor passes through Gujarat.

In the series of Vibrant Gujarat Summits it hosts, among others global partners joined officially to promote Gujarat as an International Business Hub, included United Nations Industrial Development Organisation (UNIDO), Commonwealth Business Council (CBC), and delegates from over 100 countries. In 2011 alone, Memoranda of Understanding valued at over $450 billion were signed. His admirers say Modi has placed Gujarat's development success in reaching 13,000 village centre's by globally connecting them with broadband internet through satellite technology, the largest such network in Asia.

As stated above, he has also initiated programmes to strengthen the education and health sectors, and has also reached out to enhance the role of women force in development.

"We saw the dream of parallel development of agriculture and industry a decade ago. And today in 2011 it has become a reality and is a talking point world over. That is why I say that Gujarat dreams, Gujarat delivers", retorts Modi.

"So many things work properly in Gujarat that it hardly feels like India", remarked magazine *The Economist* in its July 7th, 2011 edition. The reference is to a few glaring examples of quick delivery from the state wherein industries could set up their units and also get going. For tyre-major CEAT, it took only 24 months to get going including the normally fraught process of buying land. When the Canadian heavy machinery company Bombardier won a contract to supply compartments to Delhi Metro in 2007, it needed a factory site. It found one in Savli, an industrial estate in Gujarat in just 18 months. The speed with which things moved surprised Bombardier executives, whose managing director in India, Rajeev Jyoti has called it a "world record within Bombardier." (*The Economist*)

Needless to add, in many other parts of India, the permit process might still be grinding away. In 2008, when his project was practically shooed away from West Bengal, Ratan Tata, the head of Tata Sons, found that it took just "three days" to find a spot for a plant to build its renowned micro car, the Nano.

Among many things that investors cheer today about Gujarat are state's good roads and ports, reliable and surplus power, business-like approach of bureaucrats with less corruption and importantly the red tape kept at a distance. Therefore, Gujarat, with just five per cent of India's population, accounts for 16 per cent of the country's industrial production and 22 per cent of exports.

"Modi's strong political will and business acumen of the local bureaucrats and entrepreneurs of the state have jointly shaped investment friendly policies to unleash the potential of Gujarat", said a local businessman. Despite 2002, largely Gujarat's socio-political atmosphere remained business friendly. Moreover, the very fact that the state outshines all others in offering uninterrupted power supply, state-wide gas grid, rich gas reserves, extensive road and rail network and airports and sea ports makes it conducive for all types of investments to thrive. In effect, the business houses including from overseas hardly bother about media campaign and constant allegations from his detractors about 2002 incidents or the continuous legal battles related to 2002 cases. The corporate honchos laud the quick delivery system and dismiss alleged inaction during 2002 riots or even 'ill-action' later like Sohrabuddin encounter episode as small 'prices' to efficient and quick delivery mechanism.

"If you want to invest in India or set up plants quickly, Gujarat ought to figure at the top," rightly says Leader of the Opposition, Sushma Swaraj. In fact, her observation at

Sadbhavna Fast that when business houses approach Modi for works, they pleasantly find all relevant officials lined up in his office has many takers.

"When some business magnates enter his office, Modi is prepared with a list of yes and nos to the possible questions. Most concerned secretaries of related projects are already summoned", said a retired bureaucrat.

To questions asked umpteen times as to why investors should make a beeline to their state, the Gujarat government mandarins have pretty long answers. Some relevant check list include: Business Friendly Regulatory Environment, Simplification of Procedures, Gujarat Investor Portal, Investor Support Software, Investment Monitoring System, Industrial Zoning and Creation of Land Bank.

If the state is today attracting these unprecedented investments and trade, the Chief Minister's mantra also has a contributing factor. "Red carpet, not red tape" is what he said and has so far been able to stick to it.

Among those convinced about resurgent Gujarat, there is already excited talk about some exporters switching from China to cost-friendly India. Sanjay Lalbhai, the chairman of Arvind, a textiles maker and clothing retailer based in Ahmedabad, told *The Economist* magazine that such a move is "imminent" in his industry.

A write-up in the website First-post, titled 'Two of a kind: Why China is betting on Narendra Modi' said, "they (China) perhaps find in Narendra Modi a man that China can do business with. China's ambassador to India, Zhang Yan, reached out to Modi and expressed China's interest in working together to sharpen Gujarat's industrial and manufacturing edge, which has driven it to the top of the charts of Indian states ranked on industrialisation. He also invited Modi to visit China, which the Chief Minister said he had accepted".

The article, which was widely circulated as a newsletter from gujarat@gujaratindia.com also argued that "the Chinese invitation to Modi is an astute political move, and sends a very strong political signal, particularly in the context of the fact that Modi was in 2005 controversially denied a visa to travel to the US for his role in the 2002 riots ...... By rolling out the red carpet for Modi, in contrast to the US visa snub, Chinese officials are making a calculated investment in the future, which they know will be well received by a leader who prides himself as an embodiment of Gujarati *asmita* (self-respect)".

The article further maintained that "for Chinese leaders, Modi's involvement in the 2002 riots and his response as an administrator since then, have parallels with a defining moment in Chinese history: the 1989 massacre of student protestors and their supporters around the Tiananmen Square in Beijing. Right after the 4th June, 1989 crackdown, China faced international criticism and was subjected to sanctions". On November 9-10, 2011, Modi paid an official visit to China at the invitation of the Chinese ruling party.

The dividends from Modi's China visit would be obviously in trade and investment; but there was an important diplomatic message in this engagement with the Chinese leadership. If one takes a closer view, the visit came at a time when America's global influence is presumed to be on decline. On the other hand, experts are already talking about emergence of a new economic strength in the form of BRICS – comprising Brazil, Russia, India, South Africa and of course China.

Does it mean the stage is moving towards BRICS seeking to outsmart hitherto existing economic giants? The answer on the face value is – yes. And this statement is not given to arrogance but sheer confidence and an element of optimism. New Delhi mandarins in the Ministry of External Affairs are already calling this development as the making of a "forceful coalition" of developing countries and Indian missions are getting active to take other members into the same roadmap.

So perhaps there was a message to the establishment in

Washington from Beijing. The Communist Party of China vice chairman Wang Gang gave a warm reception to the delegation led by Modi at the Great Hall of People. The Chinese political leadership does not host Chief Ministers from India every other day. So the significance is well understood.

Besides dwelling upon the success of biennial Vibrant Gujarat Global Investors' Summit, Modi invited Chinese business delegations for the Vibrant Gujarat Summit 2013. Besides showcasing Gujarat as a destination with a suitable environment to invest and work, he also explained Gujarat becoming a major tourist destination and brought out the richness of Buddhist culture in Gujarat which solicited very keen interest among Chinese leadership. He also dwelled upon the ancient Indian and Chinese ethos, relationship, friendship, cultural and business ties. Modi had said, "To give a big boost to the economic interaction, we must emphasize on cultural exchange. I am keen to start a Mandarin language school. We also have a number of Buddhist places which can be the driver of cultural exchange". Modi stated, "I have seen growing interest among Chinese companies to work in Gujarat. We wholeheartedly welcome them. My personal visit is to reinforce that process".

Chinese Minister, International Department Cheng Fengxiang, hosted a welcome banquet in the honour of Chief Minister, and also accepted the invitation extended by the Chief Minister to visit Gujarat and agreed for China's participation in the next Vibrant Gujarat Summit in a big way. Modi offered the opportunities for collaboration in sports as Gujarat has set up a sports university. Modi also had a delegation level meeting with the Mayor of Beijing Guo Jinlong. He gave a detailed status of Gujarat and its cities as well as growing urbanization, which provides excellent opportunities for cooperation and collaboration. He invited the Mayor and his key officials to visit Gujarat and its cities to explore the cooperation and collaboration in various areas.

Simpleton behaviour, like in the rest of India, remains a principal mannerism of Gujaratis, especially in rural areas. The village has been the soul of Gujarati society though entrepreneurship had come to this state probably centuries back unlike for instance my own Bengali community. For Bengalis, 'byabsa (business)', perhaps still has a negative connotation.

But there was a perceptible change in the Gujarati social system. The business acumen of Vanias became something to be emulated by other caste groups too. Thanks to their business acumen and economic prosperity, the "pragmatism" of hardly a five per cent Vanias has virtually become synonymous with the culture of the state.

As a result, except for protecting the narrow commercial and materialistic interests, middle class and industrial class showed little interest to question – not to talk of any inclination to intervene in civic and political life.

The neo-capitalist ethos of entrepreneurship or what Gujarati baiters often say in private in city like Mumbai, "making money by hook or crook" has gained new acceptability even among backward class and in rural Gujarat. Thus the spirit of entrepreneurship is not altogether a Modi-era phenomenon but his regime has definitely given it an edge. Therefore, in the absence of any intervention in social, civil and political life, and devoid of casteist leaders like Mayawati, Mulayam Singh Yadav or Ram Vilas Paswan, even backward castes look forward to the prosperous business community (Vanias). So do Rajputs and Brahmins who also automatically follow the religious and communal lines of the neo-rich Vanias.

But it is this entrepreneurship drive that has also triggered large-scale migrations from the villages. Historically, villages are self-contained worlds, producing wheat, maize and other agri products, its artisans supplied tools and implements to farmers. But over the years, constant migration and search of better urban/modernized facilities has made Gujarat society today too largely urban-driven.

It is undoubtedly becoming more urban year by year, both demographically and culturally.

The rural population in the state in 2011 fell to 57.4 per cent from 62.6 per cent in 2001, according to state government sources while from 37.4 per cent in 2001, the urban population of Gujarat too has risen to over 42 per cent. Ahmedabad, the state's commercial hub and a trader's paradise, is the most populated district in the state, with 7.20 million people. This has also seen north-bound graph by an estimated 11.94 per cent from 2001, followed by Surat with 6.07 million people, up 10.07 per cent, as per Gujarat's Directorate of Census Operations.

It's true, both urban and rural living conditions have improved over the decades but it's only natural that this has happened unevenly. There's an estimate that the housing conditions have improved relatively more than education and health - therefore Modi government, officials say, took an unprecedented interest in bridging the gulf in these two sectors. The Chiranjeevi Yojana was launched in 2007 under which women below poverty line can go to empanelled private nursing homes for delivery and the cost for the same is borne by the state government. The state government officials say the scheme has come handy both for the people and the administration in bringing down infant and maternal mortality in Gujarat. This mechanism was necessitated as an estimated 3000 women reportedly die every year in Gujarat while delivering babies. The state infant mortality rate according to 2009 data is 48 deaths per 1000 live birth, this figure being higher than its immediate neighbour Maharashtra.

"Most of these casualties came due to delay in delivery of health services and the acute shortage of qualified gynaecologists and anaesthetists. We found Chiranjeevi Yojna very handy as the government also launched the 108 emergency ambulance service", says Jay Narayan Vyas, Health and Family Welfare Minister. According to official estimates, about 20,000 infants were born in emergency ambulances whose numbers across the state has now risen to 450. "This is a 24-hour facility and the ambulance generally arrives at 15 minutes notice", says an official.

In effect, there's a story behind the emergency ambulance service. A couple of years ago, the blockbuster film '3 Idiots' left a few health department officials in the state touched when one of the characters lament that "in this country, there's a guarantee of supplying Pizza at half an hour notice, but no such thing for ambulance". As officials spoke about the story and dropped the idea to Vyas and the Chief Minister, both readily ordered for taking necessary steps.

Dr Girish Prajapati, a Chiranjeevi Yojana Associate, was reported in an IBN7 television channel: "I approached the government for a MoU, the government gives us Rs 2.80 lakh for 100 deliveries per year. So we don't take any money from patients".

The Health Minister Vyas says the state government is taking several initiatives to make Gujarat a 'global healthcare destination' adding, there are tremendous opportunities to encourage health tourism to tap the vast potentials. "Gujarat can expect attracting more than 2 million patients in the coming few years", he says. The government also claims to have achieved excellent results from initiatives like "Bal Sakha Yojna", "Chiranjeevi Yojna" and "Extended Bal Sakha Yojna".

In yet another glaring example of innovative public-private partnership to benefit marginalised tribal farmers, Deere & Company, a world leader in the field of agricultural equipment, pledged to build a new tractor facility in Gujarat in addition to its Pune factory in Maharashtra. "This will help farmers increase their chance for prosperity and improve their quality of life", said Samuel R Allen, the Chairman and CEO of Deere & Company.

The move is aimed at making more than 500 tractors available for use by local farmers and providing the farmers access to a set of 13 different implements for various operations.

According to Modi, this public-private partnership is the first of its kind in the agriculture sector in India wherein the company would also help ensure technical skill development and enhance future employment opportunities in Gujarat by training approximately 1,000 local individuals as tractor operators.

In education and broad social indicator sectors, officials working with the Chief Minister say, the Gujarat government faced multi-pronged and very complex problems. Despite a tremendously heartening double digit GDP growth rate, there used to be huge drop out rate of children. Young students estimated about 35 per cent of rural children have malnourished and the child sex ratio was another yardstick to raise eyebrows.

The Gujarat Labour and Employment department has about 9 lakh names enrolled as unemployed youths. But like elsewhere in the country too, a bigger challenge than merely giving employment is to tackle the employability of youths. Officials admit that Gujarati local youths had missed out to benefit the initial euphoria of IT and BPO revolution as corporate found Gujarati youths not adequately qualified or conversant in English. This made the state government think of starting a finishing school type institute and also start more practical job-related courses.

The Chief Minister also took upon himself the task of visiting schools in hitherto neglected and far-flung pockets to administer tests to students to check on the quality of education being imparted. He is accompanied by a huge army of officials and volunteers. This has helped the state government undertake a more realistic task of launching the teacher-training programme in 2007. Every summer vacation, now 2-3 lakh teachers from 9000 primary schools are put through a rigorous study schedule in 4000 centres across the state to upgrade their skills. There is also a scheme for master trainers in Gandhinagar to interact with these teachers via satellite connection. For enhancing skills of talented youths in multiple disciplines, the Gujarat Skills Development Mission was set up in 2010.

Another path-breaking venture undertaken by the Modi government is on save girl child initiative. In 2005, the government had started the Beti Bachao Andolan and now the rate stands at 960 from 816 per 1000 live births in 2001. "We've made this a Jan Andolan (people's movement)", says Modi. The Chief Minister also leads the Kanya Kelavani drive, under which state officials travel in villages to encourage parents to enroll girl children into schools. According to state government officials, the initiative has resulted in rich dividends as there's a 13 per cent growth in female literacy in the state now. The female literacy rate in Gujarat is now 70 per cent, and this is higher than the national average of 65 per cent.

The Chiranjeevi Yojana in 2006 was recognised for its innovation in service delivery but a 2011 CAG report has found that the administration has missed targets. Also the number of empanelled private practitioners has fallen in some districts as clinics don't find the incentives provided by the government profitable enough to continue with the service.

Other critics say privatisation of healthcare will undermine the public healthcare system, but Modi and his council of ministers are clear: we want to put in place a system that is effective, whether it is public or private is secondary.

The change in Gujarat has not swept all parts of the state uniformly, yet there is no denying that almost every village has benefited by the developmental initiatives. The villages now have round the year and round the clock electricity with state having surplus power. About 30 per cent households in tribal areas have been given tap water supply during last five years even as in last three years farmers have been provided dedicated power supply.

The benefits of various schemes like Jyotigram Yojana and the ones mentioned above are now leaving impact of the hard work. Check dams and subsidizing expensive drip irrigation have resulted in dividends with the state able to record a 9.7 per cent agriculture growth till 2010. The broad swath along Ahmedabad-Rajkot-Surat and Baroda are perhaps best developed parts due to obvious reasons. A Planning Commission study, supported by World Bank, has said that Gujarat offers an example of international best practice in roads management.

Authored by Clell Harral, Graham Smith and William DO Paterson, the study 'Lessons from International Experience: Road Asset Management' has found four major reforms undertaken in Gujarat that make the state exemplary. These include reduced share of administrative cost in the capital and maintenance budget from 30 per cent to 16 per cent during 2000-2007; reduced maintenance backlog by half from 10,000 km to 5,000 km; increased annual plan budget for roads from $26 million in 1995-96 to $550 million in 2010-11. The latest allocation is about 9 per cent of the state planning budget as against 4 per cent in mid-nineties.

It is the unique entrepreneurship drive that has triggered large-scale migrations from the villages. Historically, villages are self-contained worlds, producing wheat, maize and other agri-products, its artisans supplied tools and implements to farmers. But over the years, constant migration and search of better urban/modernized facilities have made Gujarat society largely urban-driven. It is undoubtedly becoming more urban year by year, both demographically and culturally. Rural population has thus decreased in one way.

It's true, both urban and rural living conditions have improved over the decades but it has happened unevenly. Housing conditions have improved relatively more than education and health. Therefore, we find that the Modi regime has taken an unprecedented interest in bridging the gulf in these two sectors.

The Gujarat government is said to have earmarked 500 acres of land in Mehsana District for a car- making project. It is estimated that Maruti along with vendors could invest up to Rs 18,000 crore in Gujarat as it looks to produce around 2 million or 20 lakh units in the long run. Maruti Suzuki India is looking at a phased manner of starting car production in the state. Modi had welcomed this by saying it's a New Year gift "It's Gujarat's New Year and this is Maruti's gift to Gujarat on this occasion", Tweeted Narendra Modi after Maruti's board meeting decision to enter Gujarat.

Maruti exports around 1.38 lakh cars to Europe and Africa every year. Of these over one lakh cars are exported from a special export unit at Mundra Port. Hitherto all Maruti cars used to be manufactured in Haryana and transported by road to Mundra Port - the transportation cost per car comes up to Rs 25,000. With this new manufacturing facility in Mehsana area, Maruti is expected to save Rs 185 crore in transportation costs alone. The facility is likely to generate more than 1.50 lakh jobs.

But Modi detractors say there is much of sound and fury signifying more than what is really on the ground. Thanks to his populist announcements of schemes, the rhetoric of happiness and prosperity of peasantry and labour class is louder than the reality on the ground. There is a refrain that disparity between large and middle level farmers and small landowners and landless workers has remained unchanged if not increased. Similarly, regional disparities between irrigated areas and rain-fed areas too have increased.

However, it goes without saying that apart from gradual commercialization of agriculture and changing land system, the gradual spread of urbanization and the stitching together of urban and rural areas have also transformed Gujarat. Even far-flung and remote regions in Panchamahals district and Kutch region have been affected by urban influences through migrations, improved transportation and travel and trade. More particularly, the Kutch region of Bhuj has braved through the after-effects of the killer quake of 2001.

On 12th August, 2002, I was deputed by the Press Trust of India (PTI) to cover the then President APJ Abdul Kalam's maiden visit to Gujarat within months since he took over as the Rashtrapati. Wrapping up his two-day Gujarat visit, his first outside Delhi as the President, Dr Kalam drove down to various villages in the Kutch region, the epicenter of the quake that claimed thousands of lives. Kalam had said, "I can carry from Kutch a message for the rest of the country - that of the indomitable spirit of the people".

"When I see the type of houses built by multiple agencies, I am confident that great things are possible in the state and in the country", he had said while addressing a public meeting at the tri-junction of Bagala, Modsar and Mukhana villages about 40 km from Bhuj.

According to many admirers of Modi, the difference between small towns and villages has blurred. The thickening of village-kasba linkages has gained momentum. Old timers in rural villages near Rajkot in 2009, recollected that visiting cities like Rajkot and Ahmedabad were 'once in blue moon' experience that too by upper castes and rich and only landless migrant labourers even in early 2000. But now, several vehicles move around to and fro the cities daily full of college going students, a large number of them girls, village shoppers and a neo-brand of white collared employees.

Besides these, there are large armies of rural population now moving towards cities and small towns making as watchmen, domestic helps, truck drivers and construction workers. This, no doubt, has two sides of the same coin - good and bad.

Though migration of Gujaratis within India has been somehow limited to their established pockets like Mumbai and some neighbouring places, the international labour migration is an old phenomenon in Gujarat and was truly global. With the longest seaboard looking westward to the Middle East and Africa, Gujarat has been a land of trade and migration.

During the age of British imperialism, Gujarati businessmen sold clothes to Yemenis. In the 19th century, a large Gujarati overseas community had sprang up in British East Africa and in later stage, when America prospered, predictably Gujaratis flooded to its shores and lately also joining the bandwagon of motel proprietors and Silicon Valley software talent force.

Migration abroad for work or resettlement is a different category of mobility by choice and has always contributed to enhance Gujarati society's economic resilience. The Britishers also periodically recruited craftsmen, clerks, merchants and other professionals for settlement/employment overseas. Mahatma Gandhi to Jinnah, everybody from Gujarat has seen and worked abroad. The trend continues in manifold increase encompassing practically all professions. Most of these expatriates make handsome contribution towards Gujarat societies directly or indirectly through foreign exchange earnings. It's altogether a different chapter that over the years, overwhelming expatriates Hindus are also said to be spreading communalism back home.

In recent times, it has been experienced by many that the expatriate from the South Asian nations settled in the west or in community-sensitive countries like Australia also play a major role with regard to the growth of communalism in the region. This is best exemplified by the generous NRI funding to VHP and other Sangh organizations in the name of Ram temple movement.

In a situation like post 9/11 when the entire Muslim population has been mistaken as terrorists in the US or in Australia under a growing racial structure, fundamentalism like Hindu radicalism or hardline Muslim practices often tend to represent the national pride and identity – howsoever faulty.

Like developments everywhere, in Gujarat too, the 'development model' of Modi has its share of gainers and losers. For obvious reasons, the Modi detractors are pinning down on the losses and negativity. Losers are generally from lower strata of the society – the landless and displaced. The affected sections belonging to poorer background economically and backward castes have got marginalized and isolated in some pockets. On the contrary, the gainers are from upper echelons of the society – Patidars and those with certain assets and skill and education to capitalize on.

Another impact of socio-development change is always that the social institutions get compartmentalized and fractionated giving way to certain contradictions in social practices.

People tend to be modern, prefer pizzas but as in Gujarat they would opt for Ahmedabad's own variety of 'shudh shaka-hari' Jain pizzas and at the same hate 'meat eaters'. The loss of community also means reinforcing tendencies towards factionalism along with complete collapse of collective responsibility and welfare. Each man becomes an island of his own. These compartmentalized living also result in ghetoization of cities. Like Mumbai, a city with overwhelming Gujaratis, major Gujarat cities like Ahmedabad and Baroda are gradually getting ghettoized with 'mini Pakistan' name given to Muslim-dominated old city area very conveniently.

While, everyone makes a big issue of Modi being singularly responsible for the hyper communal image of Gujarat, a deeper analysis of the socio-political puzzles reveal that in a way Modi is also just being 'led'. Which chief minister can go against the overwhelming and near 90 per cent voice of his people?

In fact, Modi is not an exception. Even in the past, other politicians and political parties have played back to the gallery. In Ayodhya context, one can say the Congress was only trying to appeal to Hindu voters after the Shah Bano case hara-kiri. It's this which made Congress allow opening the lock at Ayodhya and then Shilanyas.

Those who expect Modi to tender an apology in 2011 for the omissions and commissions of 2002 actually look for impossibilities. In 2002 during the riot-torn days, more than once we found the common people of Gujarat and even the traders' body, Gujarat Chamber of Commerce and Industries (GCCI), had fully backed Modi and his administration for what is ostensibly held by others as non-action or inaction of the Modi government.

"The state government has stood by us," Saileshbhai Patwa, vice president of the Industry Association from Naroda Patiya, which was severely hit on the first day of the post-Godhra violence on February 28, 2002, had said.

By April 20, 2002, less than two months since the Godhra incidents the industry had suffered an estimated loss of Rs 20,000 crore - but more than anything what was visible was that - the industry here appeared to be dogged by a communal divide. The Hindu traders were backing the government. So, on the backdrop of such a situation, where is the logic in expecting Modi to tender an apology or put on a Muslim cap, which he in his wisdom declined during the *Sadbhavna* Fast.

Coming to economics, Gujarat's economy is poised to grow by double digits, even as the national rate has slowed to 7-8 per cent this year with not much prospect ahead as there is already decline in foreign direct investments due to corruption and other domestic tensions. While Congress and other detractors of Modi say development is essentially a process of survival of the Gujarati population given to immense talent in entrepreneurship. However, there are stories and allegations of crony capitalism and corruption as echoed by a former Modi aide Gordhan Zadafia and Congress leader Shaktisinh Gohil. Zadafia said there were "rampant corruption" under Modi regime and Gujarat is today being run by Dani (those who make offers), Adani and Ambani (two corporate groups). On September 15, 2011, Zadafia accompanied by few compatriots in his fledgling newly-floated outfit Maha Gujarat Janata Party, called on the President Prathiba Devi Patil against BJP leaders and Modi government's 'ill-devised' campaign against Lokayukta appointment. Later addressing a press conference at the Press Club of India, New Delhi, he said that by running away from facing a Lokayukta, the Modi government is only making itself suspicious.

He alleged gross corruption under Modi and also claimed that there were also cases of gross irregularities in land acquisition in Kutch area in the state wherein relatives of a BJP central leader have benefited much. "I quit BJP on ideological ground as the Modi government is being run only to help select corporate sector only", Zadafia had said. Zadafia, who was once a trusted lieutenant of Modi and MoS Home during 2002, also alleged gross corruption under Modi regime as reflected in CAG reports. In fact, a few days before Shaktisinh Gohil, the Leader of the Opposition in Gujarat Assembly, during his trip to Delhi had alleged that the CAG has already found irregularities to the tune of Rs 26,651 crore scam. "The Chief Minister and his men are selling precious Gujarat land and public properties to their favoured persons at throw away prices. Works are given without following tenders. People outside Gujarat do not know about these. Even Public Accounts Committee of the state assembly has found corruption in Sujlam Sufalam Project of the chief minister", he told me in an interview.

Gohil was replying to my question about the general refrain that Narendra Modi is a pro-development Chief Minister and probably also honest in financial dealings. "On the contrary Modi is the BJP's new Yeddyurappa in Gujarat. All pro-development and Vibrant Gujarat campaigns are only misleading", he had replied adding Narendra Modi knows (knew) where it pinches. "To evade these potential corruption charges against him from Lokayukta, he has referred many cases of alleged corruption to a one judge commission. The law says, if any other inquiry is being held, the Lokayukta cannot take cognizance of these cases. He is getting his insurance policy", Gohil had stated.

Here, I reproduce the interview as reported in *The Statesman*, October 15, 2011.

Interview: 'BJP is day-dreaming about Modi as PM'

The articulate Leader of the Opposition in the Gujarat Assembly, Shaktisinh Gohil, has been engaged in a fierce battle with Chief Minister Narendra Modi for the past several months. It reached a flashpoint lately when the Modi government alleged that it had been 'bypassed' by the state Governor while appointing the Gujarat Lokayukta. The issue snowballed into a major political war between the BJP and the Congress. The battle of wits intensified manifold over Mr Modi's *Sadbhavna* (harmony) Fast. Mr Gohil was recently in Delhi to present the Gujarat Congress views to the party's central leadership and the national media.

Q: You have been waging a long war against Narendra Modi in Gujarat. The dust over the Lokayukta had hardly settled when the Supreme Court ruling on the Gulberg Society case came along. The BJP is interpreting this as a clean chit for Mr Modi…

Gohil: There is no clean chit for Modi. BJP leaders are indulging in a deliberate disinformation campaign. They have bigger stakes in Gujarat.

Q: Nevertheless, the 12th September, Supreme Court ruling has also sparked off fresh speculation over Mr Modi emerging as the BJP's prime ministerial candidate in 2014…

Gohil: I know what you are referring to. The BJP leaders are also talking about advancing the Gujarat Assembly elections. About BJP making Modi its prime ministerial candidate, I can only wish them good luck. In the past, Modi has failed at the national level. During the 2009 Lok Sabha election, wherever he had campaigned, BJP candidates lost. So, the vote-catcher myth was exploded by the people of India. Indian voters are mature and politically sensitive. Modi will not be accepted as a pan-India figure and BJP leaders are only day-dreaming. Even the BJP ally, Nitish Kumar does not allow him to enter Bihar. The JD-U stayed away from Modi's *Sadbhavna* Fast. LK Advani's Rath Yatra is also aimed at addressing these questions, I suppose.

Q: How does your party view Mr Modi's fast? Mr Modi is now alleging that the state Governor is colluding with the Congress to run a parallel government. He is also planning to take the *Sadbhavna* Fast to the districts…

Gohil: The three-day *Sadbhavna* Fast was a farce. It was a five-star affair with the state government spending huge amount on it. The Governor has already sought details of the expenses from the state exchequer. Modi claimed it to be on a fast for harmony but could not generate any confidence among Muslims. He even did not bother to say sorry for the 2002 incidents.

Q: From your perspective, what is the Gujarat Lokayukta appointment controversy all about?

Gohil: As Leader of the Opposition in the Gujarat Assembly, I feel the primary controversy over the state Lokayukta's appointment stems from the BJP's double standards and its lack of ethics. It extended support to Anna movement for the Lokpal Bill, but it has another set of standards for Gujarat. This hypocrisy is disgusting. Modi himself is a champion manipulator. Last month, (August 2011) in a letter to him, I wrote in detail asking why he was shying away from appointing a Lokayukta for Gujarat. Publicly, he takes a brave posture against corruption; but in reality, he is sabotaging the Lokayukta's appointment.

Q: But the BJP said that the method of the appointment had undermined the rights and powers of the elected Cabinet system followed in the states…

Gohil: I am sorry to say that you media people get easily influenced by the rhetoric of BJP leaders. The federal structure issue is an afterthought by the BJP. It's incredible that it occurred to the BJP after so many years… the Gujarat Lokayukta Act was passed in 1986! There are valid reasons behind the provisions that define such an appointment. If Lokayuktas are appointed by Chief Ministers, how would it be possible for them to ensure that the Chief Ministers remain accountable and transparent? I have raised these issues in my letter to Modi.

Q: Has he replied?

Gohil: No, how can he? He has no answer to my questions. On the contrary, he is doing everything he can to make the Lokayukta a Chief Minister's prerogative. He is blatantly ignoring the existing laws governing the appointment of a Lokayukta. BJP leaders do not remember that their own leader Markand Desai had endorsed the current system of appointment. In fact, they implemented the same law under Keshubhai Patel and even a former BJP Chief Minister, Suresh Mehta, spoke highly of the system.

Q: But the battle is far from over. There is already a case in Gujarat High Court and BJP is making a political issue out of it...

Gohil: You are right. They have gone to court. But as you say, pending the decision of the court, they are risking contempt of court by raising a matter subjudice outside it. They are only showing utter disrespect for the constitutional offices of Governor, the Chief Justice of Gujarat High Court and the Leader of the Opposition. See, as per Clause 3 of the Lokayukta Act, the entire process of appointment has been judiciously completed. Justice RA Mehta is known as a good and fair judge. But Modi wants a man of his choice.

Q: But is the Congress not going too far? The general refrain is that Narendra Modi is a pro-development Chief Minister and probably also honest in financial dealings. But you still want to corner him over corruption charges?

Gohil: (Smiles) Actually, Modi is the BJP's new Yeddyurappa in Gujarat. All pro-development and Vibrant Gujarat campaigns are misleading. The Comptroller and Auditor-General has already found irregularities to the tune of Rs 26,651 crore. The Chief Minister and his men are selling precious land and public properties to favoured persons at throwaway prices. Contracts are being awarded without floating tenders. People outside Gujarat do not know about all this. The Public Accounts Committee of the state Assembly has detected financial irregularities in execution of the government's Sujalam Sufalam Project.

Narendra Modi knows how vulnerable he is. To ensure that the Lokayukta doesn't catch onto the irregularities, he has referred many cases of alleged corruption to a one-judge commission. The law holds that the Lokayukta cannot take cognisance of an offence if it is being already inquired into. Modi has been very particular about ensuring that he stays protected. (*The Statesman*)

Besides the corruption menace and crony capitalism, according to Modi detractors there are other critical indicators and the real story of "development and growth" in Gujarat is not quite healthy. Nearly 77 per cent of Gujarat's state population constituted by Other Backward Classes (OBCs), Dalits and Adivasis (Tribals), live in particularly marginalized and poorer conditions. The communal riots in the state since sixties have also affected the normal life of the deprived poorer sections including Dalits. Gujarat is no exception, according to this school of thought, that the controlled economic growth can only lead to disparities, unrest rather than creating an equitable society and these leading to irregular displacement of the common people. The Special Economic Zones (SEZs) and the development in ear-marked locations by acquiring land from the people by design or coercion have already hit the local communities. The vexed problem of land acquisition and the politics associated with it has also been witnessed in other parts of the country, like West Bengal and UP.

Billed as a brainchild of Manmohan Singh during his UPA-I stint, at least on paper SEZ provides for special export-promoting industrial areas with superior infrastructure facilities and also tax concessions. But skeptics say, these systems have only turned out to be the biggest land grabbing mechanism. Gujarat is probably no exception as rumour mill and allegations from rival politicians is already raising fingers on some land acquisition in the state. What experts are saying is that Gujarat's development and industrialization has also sparked off widespread displacement, especially of natives, naïve and ill-informed Adivasis.

According to one estimate, at least 6500 villages in aggregate are affected by displacement of population.

According to an authoritative study on the subject by Lancy Lobo and Shashikant Kumar for their report, 'Land Acquisition, Displacement and Resettlement in Gujarat', while in Gujarat about 15 million people were displaced during Partition in 1947, nearly 60 million have been displaced after 1947. And the displacement is obviously higher since the 1990s and even the anti-Muslim riots in 2002 led to large scale migration of the battered minority community.

There are a few other yardsticks, as claimed by a section of Modi baiters including the noted danseuse Mallika Sarabhai. In an open letter, few years back to Amitabh Bachchan, who accepted Modi's invitation to be the brand ambassador for Gujarat, she had alleged among other things that, while the all-India reduction in poverty between 1993 and 2005 is 8.5 per cent, in Gujarat it is a mere 2.8 per cent. There was debt surging high from Rs 14,000 crore debt in 2001 up to Rs 1,05,000 crore. And to service this debt, the state had to pay a whopping Rs 7,000 crore a year. She had further claimed that Gujarat's sex ratio continuously declined from 942 in 1981 to 934 in 1991 to 921 in 2001. More interestingly or rather tragically, in the 0-6 age group the sex ratio declined steeply, reaching a ratio of 600 females to 1,000 males. In the past two decades, she claimed Gujarat has been losing agricultural land at a faster rate than it did between 1960 and 1980.

"In the 49 years since it (the Narmada project) was started, and in spite of the Rs 29,000 crore spent on it, only 29 per cent of the work is complete. The construction is so poor that over the last nine years there have been 308 breaches, ruining lakhs of farmers whose fields were flooded, ruining the poorest salt farmers whose salt was washed away. Whereas in 1999, some 4,743 of Gujarat's villages were without drinking water, within two years that figure had gone up to 11,390 villages", her missive had said.

In another interesting facet of information vis-à-vis developmental works in Gujarat, the Union Minister of State for Health and Family Welfare Sudip Bandyopadhyaya on January 30, 2012 had maintained that Gujarat had higher infant mortality rate than the national average. As against the national average of 47, for Gujarat it was 48. Actually, Bandyopadhyaya was trying to defend the West Bengal government over the issue of infant deaths since for a considerable time his party government, led by irreplaceable Mamata Banerjee has been on back foot on the issue.

Generally, it is poverty that is equated with social stagnation. In the case of Gujarat, prosperity and developments brought a kind of stagnation - especially in social values. Thus, unlike any emerging and developing societies, the state of Gujarat has not been able to reconcile divergent interests of communities and their political aspirations. The element of 'outsider' and 'our own people' is so great that the state symbolizes different things to different people - ethnicities, tribes, religious and social classes.

This is partly due to a social malady also faced in the insurgency hotbed north-eastern region. There is a commonality between Gujarat and North East today; as both these places - like other states too perhaps - remain largely contested between different sets of people, their sentiments and aspirations. The craze to grow rich remains a dominant factor even among non-Gujaratis settled or pursuing jobs in Gujarat.

Therefore, when an Uttarakhandi 70 plus Hindu 'gentleman' justifies the post-Godhra 'retaliation' from Hindus in Ahmedabad, one wonders where the crux of the issue is. When we talk of a communal Gujarat, it would be criminal to consider that only native Gujaratis are turning communal. The non-Gujarati population like South Indians, UP Walla's and Bengalis of the state too are turning communal.

In Gujarat, the issue could be between Hindus and Muslims as even Assamese Muslim students were reportedly attacked during 2002 incidents. But there is no issue between Gujaratis and non-Gujaratis, for instance unlike Mumbai where north Indians come under attack from time to time.

At the peak of 2002 riots, non-Gujarati journalists flourished in the state. This writer had the first person experience; thus, I can assert with no ambiguity that there was absolute democracy for us even during the turbulent period. This is one reason Gujarat carnage got so much media attention than something similar elsewhere. Thus, I often tell my friends that the native Gujarati and outsider (Hindus from other parts of India) relationship, probably deserves a closer look.

But I would also like to point out here that, the nation-building cannot be left as an exclusive domain of the likes of Narendra Modi, the ill-motive-and-ill-advised political class and the ill-informed babus or the police force. So far, the common faceless Indians – from outside Gujarat - have also contributed sparsely little to bring Gandhi's state out of its 'hate Muslim' syndrome. We are busy blaming Modi and his party for the inaction for improving Hindu-Muslim relationship; but what about the social leadership. Now that the first move for that has not come from the state and perhaps also the local Hinduised population, barring the likes of Mallika Sarabhai, the next but crucial move to correct that ailment should come from the 'outsiders'.

This, one says in spite of the fact that several social activists from Mumbai and elsewhere are spending sleepless nights in various legal cases pertaining to the riots of 2002. But what has been happening so far is only a fierce legal battle, that too mostly outside Gujarat and gives the impression that everything including the police force and the judiciary of Gujarat are bad. It is this background that gives a room to the Gujarat government spokesman Jay Narayan Vyas to try to turn the table and assert that, "From the beginning there were certain vested interests who never wanted victims to get justice, and these elements are working hard to obstruct the judicial process by various means and to give a political tint to this case (Ehsan Jafri case). Such important cases have seen a stay of six years because of the hindrance of these elements". In the ultimate, answers too many of these questions about Gujarat remain in the womb of time.

Probably, it would not be wrong to say that it's likely that 5 or 10 years from now the multitude of social sector schemes launched by the Modi regime in the last couple of years or facilitated by a riot-tainted regime will show results. But Modi's real test awaits him in 2012 end when Gujarat goes to polls and Modi fights for his fourth term as Chief Minister.

Chapter - 5

A Legacy of Litigations

When Narendra Modi sat on a three-day fast in Gandhinagar,. it was rightly rumoured that there are two sets of people - one who approve of Narendra Modi and the other, those who do not. In Gujarat, the numbers are overwhelmingly in favour of Modi and elsewhere it all depends on which side of the dividing line one puts oneself. Over the last decade Modi has truly weathered enough brickbats and political discomfort. LK Advani says he does not know of any politician, who has been wrongly vilified like Modi. Ironically, in May 2012, he was not happy Modi stealing the limelight in Mumbai convention of the party.

Most of these are Modi's own making and the remaining is due to the highly communal frenzy in Gandhi's Gujarat and at the same time the obsession of the secular brigade about the state and its leader since 2002.

The worst of all for Modi came in the form of a series of fierce legal battles. The Best Bakery case of Baroda, Ehsan Jafri murder case of Gulberg Society in Ahmedabad, the IPS officer Sanjiv Bhatt case, Naroda Patiya besides the various commissions and SITs into different cases like the encounters are permanent news stories in legal and often in front pages in the media for last ten 10 years.

Best Bakery case

The Best Bakery case had snowballed into a major politico-legal controversy with the Supreme Court ordering reopening of the trial of the case in Mumbai from 2003. All the 22 accused in the case were acquitted by a Vadodara (Baroda) fast track court due to lack of evidence.

The transfer of the case was felicitated after the National Human Rights Commission (NHRC) petitioned the Supreme Court for a fresh trial of Best Bakery case along with four other cases. The Commission's steps came more than a month after the fast-track court in Gujarat had ordered acquittal of 22 accused in the case. Prior to that on July 7, 2003, a key witness and daughter of the bakery owner Zaheera Habibullah Shaikh at a press meet at Press Club in Mumbai had demanded that the case should be reopened and tried "outside Gujarat".

Zaheera said she was threatened with life from an influential BJP leader and was scared to go back to her native place. Zaheera, then 19, had lost six members of her family including her father during the infamous March 1, 2002 Best Bakery incident as one of the numerous first post-Godhra anti-Muslim violence. The incident had claimed 14 lives.

The four other cases, which NHRC sought to be transferred are the Godhra February 27 inferno, Chamanpura's Gulberg Society incident, Naroda Patiya killing and Sadarpura incident in Mehsana district. Notably, by 2010-11 all these cases again resurfaced as breaking news and in front pages.

Ordering the transfer of the case to Mumbai, one of the Supreme Court judges had, as stated earlier in this book too, said "The modern day Neros were looking elsewhere when Best Bakery and innocent children and helpless women were being burnt....".

I was in Mumbai those days working for the city-based popular daily, *The Free Press Journal*. As news coordinator of the reporting team, I gave upon myself the task of tracking the case a major assignment.

Hardly a year and four months since her media appearance and demand for transfer of the Best Bakery case re-trial outside Gujarat, the star eye-witness Zaheera Sheikh made a volte face in November 2004 and had alleged that social activist Teesta Setalvad had been threatening and pressurizing her.

At a press conference at Vadodara (Baroda), Zaheera had alleged that she was detained in a Mumbai hotel by the social activist Teesta of Mumbai-based Citizens for Justice and Peace for seven months and was pressurized to implicate a certain individual in the case. Teesta had obviously denied the charges and also filed an application in the Supreme Court seeking a CBI probe into the circumstances which led Zaheera to revert back from her earlier public statement.

Zaheera had made the statement before the media and outside court at Vadodara without any oath sparking off debate whether her statement should be taken on record by the special court of additional sessions judge Abhay Thipsay. What raised further eyebrows was that Zaheera had moved out of a rented flat at Yari Road in Mumbai reportedly arranged by Teesta and had subsequently moved to Mira Road in the suburbs of western Mumbai in early 2004.

Zaheera's statement had not only turned the table against Teesta and presumably to an extent against the prosecution after the witnesses had identified three accused, but a virtual Pandora's Box was let open as her brother Nasibullah had also added to the prosecution woes by escaping from a guest house in Mumbai.

Even the examination of Zaheera's sister-in-law Yasmin Sheikh was postponed on November 5, 2004 with the defence lawyer pleading about his tooth ache. On the other hand, the public prosecutor Manjula Rao expressed concern on this and at one point even wondered, "What if Yasmin also turns out to be somewhat like Zaheera". The case was turning curious by every hour outside the court and by every deposition in the court.

Zaheera had claimed that Yasmin Sheikh had already been divorced by her brother while another accused Dinesh Rajbhar claimed in the court that Teesta had threatened him too saying, "*.... Tum sab ko dekh lenge*". Rajbhar was earlier identified by a witness Rais Khan as being part of the mob.

On November 1, 2004, Rais had recalled that on the fateful day of the incident at Vadodara in March 2002, as retaliation to Godhra station inferno, a group of 15 rioters had come to the vicinity of the bakery and pelted stones and later at night the mob had again come despite curfew with most activists holding sword and burning torches (*mashal*).

Later on June 12, 2006, finding Zaheera Sheikh guilty of giving false evidence in the Best Bakery case, a sessions court in Mumbai had sentenced her to three months rigorous imprisonment (RI) and asked her to pay a fine of Rs 500. The three-month sentence would begin after Zaheera completes the one year jail term she was undergoing for committing contempt of court. Judge Abhay Thipsay also ordered Zaheera to undergo 10 days of additional jail term in case of default for payment of fine.

The judge found Zaheera guilty of giving false evidence on 15 counts. Earlier, the court had sentenced her mother Sahrunisa, and sister Sahira to three months' rigorous imprisonment and fined them Rs 500 each on similar charges. Both were though granted bail. Zaheera's brother Nasibullah, who, too, was found guilty of perjury, was put on probation because of his young age.

Gulberg Society case

A high-profile case, the Gulberg Society inferno happened on February 28, 2002 in Ahmedabad. Zakia Jafri, wife of Ehsan Jafri, lodged a complaint on June 8, 2006 alleging that the police had not registered the FIRs against Narendra Modi and 62 others including several ministers for the infamous inferno of February 28, 2002 in Ahmedabad. She alleged that there was a well-planned conspiracy to allow the massacre of Muslims in which policemen and bureaucrats were ordered not to respond to pleas for help from the victims. She approached the Gujarat High Court with her complaint, which on November 3, 2007, refused to entertain her plea, and instead asked her to present the case before magistrate's court. Subsequently, she approached the Supreme Court which on April 27, 2009 appointed a five-member Special Investigation Team (SIT), headed by former CBI head RK Raghavan, to probe these cases and asked the SIT to look into her complaint of collusion of the state machinery and the rioters.

On September 12, 2011, the Supreme Court, perhaps for the first time since the trial into various Gujarat-related cases, gave a sort of reprieve to the beleaguered Modi government. It directed a trial court in Gujarat to take a final decision on the complaint of Zakia Jafri, and thereby rejected the plea from the petitioner to make the Chief Minister and sixty-two others a direct party in the case. Zakia had charged Modi and others with orchestrating the post-Godhra violence in connivance with senior police and civil officials. Sixty-nine people were killed when the Gulberg Society housing colony in Ahmedabad was attacked on February 28, 2002. The Supreme Court, on March 26, 2008, ordered the Narendra Modi government to re-investigate 10 cases in the 2002 Gujarat riots, including the Gulberg Society incident. In March 2010, Gulberg Society case trial was stayed by the Supreme Court after the special public prosecutor RK Shah resigned after accusing the trial judge and SIT of being "soft on the accused". Activist Teesta Setalvad, in an affidavit filed before the Supreme Court in April 2010, submitted phone-record analysis claiming that the then Ahmedabad Police Commissioner PC Pande had spoken to Joint Commissioner of Police MK Tandon six times during the period when the latter was present at Gulberg Society and the mob was growing restive. However, due to some questionable reasons the police did not act to disperse a riotous mob of angry Hindus, a day after Godhra train inferno.

Predictably, as the news of the Supreme Court directive on September 12, 2011 started breaking on television channels, the BJP was quick to jump to the conclusion that the court verdict had given their much cornered Chief Minister the much needed clean chit. The party veteran LK Advani was among the first to react stating "the court has given a crushing reply to all those who vilified and maligned Modi for almost 10 long years". Modi himself in his tweet, said, "God is Great" while Sushma Swaraj also twitted saying Modi has passed the 'agniparikshah'. The Congress and the Left, as expected, screamed that BJP was jumping the gun with Congress party spokesman and a lawyer by profession Abhishek Singhvi pointing out that the court has "not opined on the merits of the case, directly or indirectly".

Zakia Jafri was in pensive mood saying she was "disappointed" lamenting, "What should I expect from the lower court if I did not get justice from the Supreme Court".

The Gujarat cabinet spokesman Jay Narayan Vyas was much elaborate in his response, "Good news for those having faith in the Constitution of India is that the apex court's verdict has completely rooted out the serious allegation that was levelled at Gujarat government". In a detailed statement Vyas said, "Certain elements having vested interest, wanted to subvert the Gujarat government by making FIR against the Chief Minister and government officials. But the Supreme Court did not let succeed such malicious motives and rejected the demand of lodging FIR. Elements with political interest made strenuous efforts to entrust the probe to CBI but the Supreme Court has once again expressed confidence on SIT quashing the demand for CBI inquiry. These people leaved no stone unturned in throwing mud on the judiciary of Gujarat. But the Supreme

Court has expressed full confidence in the judicial process of Gujarat and has directed the concerned court to deal with the case.

"Supreme Court's verdict that there is no need to monitor the functioning of SIT proves that the apex court has complete trust on SIT. People of Gujarat know that the Chief Minister of the state always prefers to be lawabiding. The government of Gujarat once again expressed its commitment to get justice to the victims. Wish that those playing narrow politics learn a lesson from this".

Amid drumbeats and distribution of sweets in BJP circles, the word also quickly started spreading that this 'relief' from the apex court would pave the way to put Modi as a frontrunner in the national level vis-à-vis the candidature of prime ministership in 2014 polls. "As long as the matter was under active consideration of the Supreme Court, the sword of Damocles was hanging over Modi's head", said *The Hindu* in a front-page story. In quick response, Modi also announced his three-day *Sadbhavna* (goodwill) fast, which was rightly, billed Modi's "fast-track" towards Delhi. "But things are still too early", plainly summed up a magazine writer for Shillong-based *Eastern Panorama*. "A section of BJP leaders privately admit about the limitations of Modi brand in national politics. Though hyped more than once, Modi has failed to ensure victory for BJP candidates outside Gujarat", the magazine said. In fact, many see pragmatism in this analysis.

Advani's rejection in 2009 was probably due to hardliner Hindutva image as compared to Vajpayee's pan-Indian acceptability. In 2009, Manmohan Singh was the middle-class hero for his moderate image. BJP watchers say, Modi campaigned even in Assam assembly polls in 2011, but the result was failure. Earlier, in 2004 polls, his campaign did not yield dividends to the party in Himachal Pradesh and in parliamentary polls, it was rather voted out. Even in Gujarat, BJP's performance in both Lok Sabha polls - 2004 and 2009 - were not good.

In March 2012, after the UP election results; observers were again found working overtime analyzing how Akhilesh Yadav's sober and humble approach could help him storm to power in UP as against an attempt made by Rahul Gandhi to present himself as an angry young man – either pulling up sleeves or tearing the election manifestoes. In my dispatch for *The Statesman* on March 6, 2012, the day of counting, I had said: "Unlike several other socialist politicians from the cow-belt, Akhilesh concentrated more on ground work and work at grassroots instead of bravado of the likes of Lalu Prasad or segmented appeal of Ram Vilas Paswan in Bihar. He did not have lung power of the political class of the cow-belt but he spoke more what really made sense for the electorate. Even his political rivals and old war horses like Arun Jaitley of BJP have on record appreciated his sober and more sensible approach in contrast to Congress chief campaigner Rahul Gandhi's symbolic gestures of tearing off the manifestoes".

Thus, the message was that people would prefer a humble and down to earth approach in contrast to bravado. So Modi perhaps runs another test case of a stiff competition from Nitish Kumar.

Therefore, the bigger issue remains: Gujaratis too could prefer him and BJP in the state; but not the same saffron party at the national level. Thus, the moot question still is, can Modi emerge as a vote-catcher nationwide.

Timeline: Gulberg Society Case

February 28, 2002: Gulberg Society, a cluster of 29 bungalows and 10 apartment buildings housing upper middle class families mostly belonging to the Muslim community in Ahmedabad was attacked by a Hindu mob, which breached the boundary wall and started torching houses. By evening, 69 people, including former Congress MP Ehsan Jafri were killed.

June 8, 2006: Zakia Jafri, wife of Ehsan Jafri, submits a complaint to be lodged alleging that the police had not registered the FIRs against Narendra Modi and sixty-two others including several ministers and high ranking officials of the state administration. However, the police have refused to lodge the complaint.

November 3, 2007: The Gujarat High Court refused to entertain her plea, and instead asked her to present the case before Magistrate's Court.

March 26, 2008: The Supreme Court ordered the Narendra Modi government to re-investigate 10 cases in the 2002 Gujarat riots, including the Gulberg Society incident. The court created a SIT, headed by ex-CBI Director RK Raghavan to probe the cases afresh.

March, 2009: The Supreme Court asked the SIT to look into Zakia's complaint for collusion of the state machinery and the rioters and also the role of the Chief Minister and others mentioned in the complaint.

September 2009: Supreme Court lifts stay on the trial of most important cases including the Gulberg Society case, so trial begins.

March 27, 2010: SIT summoned Gujarat Chief Minister Narendra Modi to clarify things. Modi was grilled for several hours regarding his alleged action or lack of it during the riots.

March 2010: Gulberg Society case trial was stayed by the Supreme Court after the special public prosecutor RK Shah resigned after accusing the trial judge and SIT of being "soft on the accused".

May 14, 2010: The Special Investigative Team (SIT) finally submitted its report to the registry.

March 11, 2011: Supreme Court asks the SIT to look into the doubts raised by *amicus curiae* Raju Ramchandran, who had replaced Prashant Bhushan as *amicus curiae.*

June 18, 2011: Ramchandran visited Ahmedabad and met material witnesses and others to prepare his report on the SIT's report.

July 25, 2011: Ramchandran submitted his report to the Apex Court.

July 28, 2011: Supreme Court decides to keep the report confidential and declined to allow access to the Gujarat government and the SIT.

September 12, 2011: Supreme Court directs the trial court to decide whether Modi and others can be probed. The court has also decided to cease monitoring the case and no time-frame set for the trial court.

SIT-Raghavan report

On February 8, 2012, the SIT headed by R Raghavan filed a sealed final report on Gulberg Society riot in Ahmedabad Metropolitan Court. The SIT report presumably found no prosecutable evidence against all fifty-six people including Chief Minister Narendra Modi. The SIT report predictably got mired in controversies for more than one reason. In the closure report, the SIT said, ".... Narendra Modi has clearly stated in his Zee TV interview that it was late Jafri, ex-MP, who first fired at violent mob and the provoked mob stormed the Society and set it on fire. In this interview, he has clearly referred to Jafri's firing as 'action' and the killings that followed as 'reaction'. It may be clarified here that in case late Jafri, ex-MP, fired at the mob, this could be an immediate provocation to the mob, which had assembled there to take revenge of Godhra incident from the Muslims". The SIT also justified Modi's description of Godhra residents as people with "criminal tendencies" and it said, with regard to the Godhra incident, (Modi) clearly stated that the day before yesterday forty ladies and children were burnt alive at Godhra and the incident had shocked the nation as well as people abroad, and that the people belonging to this area had a criminal tendency and these people had earlier killed lady teachers and now they had committed heinous crime for which the reactions were being felt".

The SIT report among other things maintained that the allegation that Modi issued a "directive" to police officers to "allow Hindus to vent their anger" had "not been established". It further concluded that police officer Bhatt was an "unreliable witness" and that it was not confirmed either the then Minister of State for Revenue Haren Pandya was present at the meeting. It contested the view that Modi's personal decision was meant to inflame the situation by "parading the bodies" of Godhra carnage as he argued that the bodies were brought in the dead of night and disposed of in the quickest possible time the next day. The SIT also concluded that there was nothing to substantiate the charge that two senior Ministers were "instructed" by the Chief Minister to take charge of the State and city police control rooms on February 28, 2002, when 'Gujarat Bandh' was observed. It maintained that though the late Ashok Bhatt, who was Health Minister, and IK Jadeja, the then Urban Development Minister, did visit the police control rooms, but there was no evidence that they ever 'interfered' with the functioning of the police. It also could not be confirmed that they were told by the Chief Minister to sit in the control rooms. Raghavan's report also pooh-poohed the charge that there was undue delay in summoning and deploying the Army in the riot-hit areas. The report also did not agree that Modi was issuing any instruction orally or otherwise, as alleged by the former Additional Director-General of Police, RB Sreekumar, in affidavits filed before the GT Nanavati-Akshay Mehta Judicial Inquiry Commission. SIT maintained that Sreekumar's personal diary in which he reportedly made entries about such "illegal oral instructions" was an "unofficial document" he was not authorised to maintain. However, the report said the transfer of a few police officers amid the raging riots, especially those who were claimed to have done a good job in controlling the violence, were surprising, but none of the police officers was prepared to admit that they were victimised.

The suspended IPS officer Sanjiv Bhatt in his reaction wrote a rather angry letter to Raghavan and lamented that it was "outrageously shocking" that the SIT had functioned "with the sole purpose and motive of shielding Mr Modi and other powerful accused persons from legal punishment".

There was also allegation about RK Raghavan, who headed the Special Investigation Team, that he had compromised his role in investigating the case by accepting a favour like funding for his London trip. Raghavan denied the charges. "On both occasions I travelled to Ahmedabad to attend to Supreme Court-ordered work at great personal inconvenience interrupting my other responsibilities. Although I was entitled to Executive Class travel on SIT work, I travelled Economy from London to Ahmedabad and back to London on both the occasions. My return air ticket cost me less than Rs 40,000 each time. On the other hand, if I had travelled from Chennai [instead from London] to Ahmedabad and got back to Chennai after attending to SIT work by Executive Class [which I normally do when I am in India] that would have cost the state government about Rs 65,000 each time. This means that I saved the government Rs 50,000 on the two trips I made to Ahmedabad from London by travelling economy. To say that the State government favoured me by sending me to London is mischievous and utter falsehood with a view to maligning me, and that too when I am abroad and without checking facts from me or the Gujarat government," Raghavan said. (*The Hindu*, March 15, 2012)

Staged Encounter: Ishrat case

The Gujarat police and the state government came in for much more embarrassment with regard to June 15, 2004 so-called 'encounter killing' of supposed four Lashkar-e-Taiba terrorists. On December 1, 2011, the Gujarat High Court handed over the Ishrat Jehan murder case to the CBI. In a serious indictment of the police establishment in the state, a Division Bench of the Gujarat High Court, comprising Justices Jayant Patel and Abhilasha Kumari, said the Gujarat state police could not be trusted for the probe.

Ishrat, a 19-year-old college girl who hailed from Mumbra on the outskirts of Mumbai near Thane, along with Javed Sheikh *alias* Pranesh Pillai, Amjad Ali Rana and Zeeshan Johar was killed in a shootout by Ahmedabad Crime Branch on June 15, 2004.

Earlier on November 21, 2011, the High Court had accepted the report of the Special Investigation Team (SIT) appointed by the Gujarat High Court. The report filed by three-member SIT headed by Bihar-cadre IPS officer Rajiv Ranjan Verma had concluded that contrary to the claims by the Gujarat police, among other things, not a single cartridge from the 70 rounds the police claim to have fired in self-defence was recovered from the scene. Moreover, the bullet holes in cars at scene contradict police account of encounter.

In June 2004, Ahmedabad police had claimed that they shot dead four Lashkar-e-Taiba terrorists on a mission to assassinate Narendra Modi, which now SIT says – was entirely staged and the teenaged girl from Mumbra, a student of Mumbai's Khalsa College, and three men, who died with her were 'murdered' by policemen in cold blood.

Like yet another controversial encounter of Sohrabuddin, this is the second time the Gujarat police's claim to have saved their Chief Minister from assassination could not buy conviction at the end of the day. In its order of December 1, the court while transferring the case to CBI said that the police officer Satish Verma, who was a member of the SIT, could provide assistance to the CBI.

Sadly, pending final report from the CBI, it is now indicated that the four were in police custody earlier and killed at some other place and time, and the bodies were dumped on the road near Kotarpur, on the outskirts of Ahmedabad, in the early hours of June 15, 2004. Earlier, a routine judicial inquiry into the encounter, conducted by Ahmedabad Metropolitan Magistrate SP Tamang, had also concluded in his report submitted on September 7, 2009 that the encounter was fake and they were 'executed in cold blood by the police officials for their benefit'.

Sanjiv Bhatt: The man against Modi

Another major legal battle vis-à-vis the politics of Gujarat and Modi pertains to the affidavit filed by suspended IPS officer Sanjiv Bhatt.

Bhatt was arrested by Gujarat police on September 30, 2011 on a complaint filed in June (2011) in Ahmedabad's Ghatlodiya police station by a police constable KD Panth. The complainant had alleged that Sanjiv Bhatt had threatened and forced him (Pant) to sign a false affidavit before the Supreme Court appointed *amicus curiae* (officer of the court) in support of Sanjiv Bhatt's claim that in a high-level meeting on February 27, 2002, the Chief Minister had directed the police officials to "allow Hindus to vent their anger (for Godhra train blaze) on the Muslims".

A 1988 batch IPS officer, Bhatt, is a quintessential fighter as well as one of most media-friendly cops in Gujarat. Probably, no journalist who has worked in Ahmedabad for a brief period would not know him or has not taken the benefit of his 'help' in terms of getting the 'right and police' version (information) about things happening in the state.

I am one person, who ought to have the necessary gratitude for all his help from the day I happened to know him. My first interaction with Bhatt was over phone after I managed to get in touch with his office at Gandhinagar, courtesy my fellow journalist friends Thomas Kutty Abraham and Anosh Malekar. "Let's meet up sometime," was his open invitation and I, like scores of other journalists deputed to cover country's toughest assignment of circa 2002, started counting Bhatt as a 'friend' and a 'reliable source', to use the journalistic cliché. 'Sanjiv Sahab', he disapproved being called 'Bhatt Sahab', would often go out of the way to help provide us the information we were looking for. During 2002, one of the stories I broke was about a large number of Muslim youths getting their act together to float 'Lashkar-e-Khaladeen'. Bhatt was one of the men who put me on the track to get hold of the story. As we started knowing him gradually, various facets of his qualities and perhaps also a certain weaknesses started coming to light. But all said, in short, he was one of my "favourites" among the sources I had in Ahmedabad especially during the tough assignment of covering Gujarat in 2002 that too for a highly demanding news organization, the Press Trust of India.

He was again a true friend, who came to my aid when I landed in Ahmedabad on September 23, 2002, the day Akshardham temple in Gandhinagar was attacked by two terrorists. By then Bhatt, alleged to have ruffled Modi regime, was already transferred out of the crime branch. But the moment I called him seeking information on the terror attack and other details; his response was typical of Sanjiv Bhatt characteristic: "I am nobody now; but you are my friend from Mumbai and I promise I will help you".

Needless to add, the information flew in. Later his wife Shwetta once told me, "Sanjiv sat near the phone and kept on collecting information for you from junior guys. He said he could not say no to his *babu moshai*" (The last phrase is reference to my being a Bengali).

Even otherwise, I found a typical 'Mumbaikar-like' helpful approach in him. And why not? He was born in Mumbai and had his education from IIT, Bombay. "As a Mumbai man, I would always cherish your association. That city knows how to stay together, the pluralism and so on ..... and look what has happened to Ahmedabad," he had told me in April 2002. A bright student, Bhatt should have been otherwise making news as the one of the first IPS officers among Gujaratis. Bhatt has made news for reasons best known to him – right or wrong. He is stuck to the rank of superintendent of police for over a decade and now his promotion seems unlikely for all obvious reasons.

He is said to have provoked anguish from the political class in general and not just Modi alone. Therefore, the latest round of controversy he is in is not quite surprising for those who know Sanjiv Bhatt. In 2003, as the Superintendent of Sabarmati Central Jail, Bhatt was alleged to have turned too friendly with prisoners. That was perhaps the beginning of his long-drawn battle with the Modi establishment. Now, the Modi government seems to have engaged itself in a full-time battle with the suspended cop. Five days after his arrest, in an affidavit filed in the court of Justice VK Vyas of Gujarat High Court, investigating officer NC Patel said, Bhatt has a "criminal behaviour/ways".

Stating that there are number of criminal cases registered against Bhatt in Gujarat, the affidavit prayed that his bail should not be granted. It mentioned the 1990 case of police atrocity against Bhatt in Jamnagar district, a case of custodial torture in 1994 at Porbander, and a 1996 case under Narcotics Drugs and Psychotropic Substance (NDPS) Act in Pali, Rajasthan.

The affidavit further said that Bhatt as an 'influential person' could intimidate witnesses in the '2002 Narendra Modi-meeting top police officials' case by threatening them.

Till Bhatt had filed his affidavit, the 'secret' meeting the Chief Minister purportedly held was only whispered about. But former DGP KK Chakravarthi has denied about Bhatt's presence in the meeting saying, he was too junior to be called in that meeting. KD Pant in his affidavit earlier said that he had dropped Bhatt at the Chief Minister's residence for the meeting.

However, another senior police officer, the former ADG, CID, RB Sreekumar had also claimed in his personal diary noting that in that meeting on February 27; Modi had asked the law and order machineries to 'go slow' on the arsonists. There are also reports that Modi's *bête noire* in state politics, the late Haren Pandya had testified before a tribunal and he too had spoken about Modi's seemingly justification of Hindus anguish against the Muslims. As mentioned above, these claims have been, however, dismissed by the SIT report of RK Raghavan.

Earlier, on April 22, 2011, Bhatt, then Principal of the State Reserve Police Training College, Junagadh, had filed an affidavit in the Supreme Court stating that Chief Minister Narendra Modi had directed top police officers on the eve of the 2002 incidents to "allow the Hindus to vent their anger" and "teach a lesson" to Muslims. He also had accused the Supreme Court-appointed Special Investigation Team of trying to "cover up the larger conspiracy and official orchestration" behind the riots.

Bhatt had claimed that the police control room had conveyed to him about the meeting to be presided over by the Chief Minister and that he was instructed to attend the same as his immediate senior the then Additional Director-General of Police, Intelligence, GC Raigar was on leave. Bhatt was SP rank official and Deputy Commissioner of Intelligence in the State Intelligence Bureau, Gandhinagar, and the post he held from December 1999 to September, 2002. According to him, whose testimony was recorded by the SIT, "Narendra Modi said [at the February 27 meeting] that the bandh call had already been given, and the party [the BJP] had decided to support the same, as incidents like the burning of kar sevaks at Godhra could not be tolerated".

He further impressed upon the gathering that for too long, the Gujarat police had been following the principle of balancing the actions against the Hindus and Muslims while dealing with communal riots. This time, the situation warranted that the Muslims be taught a lesson to ensure that such incidents do not recur ever again. The Chief Minister, Mr Modi, expressed the view that the emotions were running very high amongst the Hindus, and it was imperative that they be allowed to vent out their anger", the affidavit stated. (*The Hindu*)

Bhatt said the effects of Modi's "directions" widely manifested in the "half-hearted approach and lack of determination" on the part of the police in dealing with the "orchestrated violence". Curiously, Bhatt also had claimed that the SIT, however, had refused to accept his line and was allegedly reluctant to examine the existence of any larger conspiracy behind the riots.

But the Modi camp has made light of these charges. The refrain from the camp is that vested interest elements, wanting to arouse the anger of the victims and to plot political games, resorted to making a series of false allegations. "Even years after in order to settle political accounts, they made false allegations on the Gujarat government including the Chief Minister", is one refrain from Modi's camp.

Bhatt, as I know and as all indications suggest, is the last man to give up the struggle. "Let them do their job and let me do mine...," he said in initial reactions walking out of the jail on bail on October 17, 2011. He has among other things alleged that the raid conducted in his house even without mandatory information to his wife was only aimed at destroying important evidence against Modi.

The Gujarat government is going full steam against Bhatt. On October 22, 2011, the state CID brought in charges of financial irregularities against Sanjiv Bhatt and a retired IPS officer, RMS Brar. The police said a scam of Rs 20 crore was related to the period between 2006 and 2010, when Bhatt was posted in the State civil defence department under Brar, the Additional Director-General of Police, who retired in 2010. According to police, the civil defence department had requisitioned purchase of some sirens to be installed in all the district and taluka headquarters for cautioning people during any emergency or an impending natural disaster. A purchase committee was set up to decide on the tenders submitted.

The committee had rejected a Bangalore-based company's tender because it had been earlier black-listed by the Centre. This purchase was supposed to be felicitated by central funding of 75 per cent. The department authorities had bypassed the report of the committee and recommended the same Bangalore-based company to Mr Brar, who then approved the deal. Some 500 sirens were purchased from the company at a cost of over Rs 20 crore.

In 2010, the state home department had ordered a probe and now it seemed the inquiry revealed some foul play alleging "financial irregularities" in the purchase of sirens by Bhatt and Brar.

Thus, the cases related to Sanjiv Bhatt are only turning complex and curious. By mid-October, 2011, Gujarat Pradesh Congress Committee (GPCC) president Arjun Modhwadia was apprehensive of his arrest in the Bhatt case.

Even as the Congress has blasted at the Modi regime for trying to politicize Sanjiv Bhatt case, Modhwadia himself penned an open letter to the Chief Minister stating, "Though I am an elected representative of the Gujarat Assembly and a law-abiding citizen of Gujarat you disregarded everything to get my telephone records to snoop on me. This is a serious breach of my privacy and I have complained to you about this earlier too".

He also alleged that in 2002, if the state government had provided adequate security to the Ram Sevaks at Godhra railway station, the state could have been saved from experiencing such a big tragedy like communal riots. "Instead, according to Bhatt's affidavit before the Supreme Court, you asked the state police to refrain from stopping the unbridled rioting", the Congress leader wrote.

On October 17, 2011 after days of fierce legal battle, Bhatt walked out of the Sabarmati central jail to an enthusiastic welcome after he was granted bail by judge VK Vyas. Walking out of the jail, Bhatt told waiting journalists that this was just the beginning of his battle – "the cause I am fighting is bigger than me". In the interim period when he was behind bars, the IPS Officers' Association had expressed solidarity with him and also visited his house. But the Modi government is not keen to give it up either. By next two days; the state government brought in another Section 120 (b) of the Indian Penal Code. This meant adding the charge of 'conspiracy' against Bhatt for his purported claim that he was present during the Chief Minister's meeting with senior police officials on February 27, 2001. It was understood in legal circles that adding of the new charge could create fresh problems for Bhatt and also create problem for Congress state president Arjun Modhwadia. In all these, however, the government spokesman Jaynarayan Vyas had claimed that the government had no hand and the normal probe was on, purely on the basis of a personal complaint from Constable KD Panth.

Besides the new charge of 'conspiracy'; the government has also slapped another case on Bhatt in the form of a 21-year-old custodial death of a VHP activist at Jamjodhpur when Bhatt was posted as Assistant Superintendent of Police in Jamnagar district. It was in 1990 when 140 people were arrested at Jamjodpour following communal problem in the aftermath of LK Advani's arrest in Bihar when his famous Rath Yatra was stopped from moving beyond by the Lalu Prasad government there. Among them one VHP activist died after his release. The family members of the deceased Prabhudas had filed complaint against Bhatt and six other policemen claiming that the VHP activist had succumbed to his injuries sustained during police custody. But all these were not surprising perhaps to Gujarat watchers and also the police officer Bhatt.

In his own words: "I will do my work and they will do theirs. I am not going to leave them and they would also not leave me", Bhatt had said. The Bhatt case had come before the Supreme Court on November 18, 2011 with the police official seeking the apex court's intervention and sought a ruling so that he is not prosecuted in the alleged custodial death of VHP activist. The Bench of Justices BS Chauhan and TS Thakur made it clear that he could seek remedy in the session's court. Appearing for Bhatt, senior counsel, Gopal Subramaniam submitted that there were factual inaccuracies in the case as it was not a case of custodial death per se. On this Justice Chauhan remarked that all these issues could be decided only at the trial court.

In Delhi, in November 2011 on bail, suspended cop lamented that Gujarat had turned to be a "laboratory of hatred politics". He drew similarity between 1984 anti-Sikh riots and 2002 Gujarat riots and sought to clarify that he has not been raising the issue with any motivate against BJP or Modi. He said in the ultimate, it is the common man who bears the brunt as most communal violence is politically motivated. "Public never want riot. It is the poor Hindu or the poor Muslim who gets perished", Bhatt had remarked.

There are, however, some individuals who have persistent differences with Sanjiv Bhatt. Past mid-night April 19, 2012, on Facebook, one Vinod Mirani wrote: "Sanjiv

Bhatt, you should have risen against whatever wrong was happening instantly, not after a decade of slumber; may be you could have stopped it!"

Bhatt was predictably annoyed and he too responded sharply: "You are making these statements because you are not aware of the facts. I and my the then boss in the Intelligence Bureau, RB Sreekumar, and IPS had fully discharged our constitutional duty during the Gujarat riots. Both of us were transferred by a common order in September 2002. People like you need to come out of the comfort zone of ignorance and indifference".

However, table seems to be turning with the report of Raju Ramachandran, the *amicus curiae* in the Zakia Jafri case. Even before the reports came out in public knowledge, and taken note by the court, media report claimed that it has "laid the ground for Narendra Modi to be charge-sheeted", for his alleged role in the 2002 anti-Muslim riots. "If the trial court accepts Ramachandran's view, the sources said, the stage will have been set for the prosecution of the Chief Minister under various sections of the IPC, among them, 153 A (statements promoting enmity between communities), 153 B (imputations and assertions prejudicial to national integration) 505 (statements conducing to public mischief) and 166 (public servant disobeying a direction of the law with the intent to cause injury)," claimed a report in *The Hindu*.

When the report came to light, it did contradict the SIT Raghavan report and said Modi could be charge-sheeted.

In para 24, the report by Raju Ramachandran said, "I also find it difficult to accept the conclusion of the SIT that Bhatt's statement is motivated, because he has an axe to grind with the State government over issues concerning his career. Further, in my opinion, it may not be proper to disbelieve Bhatt at this stage, only because the other officers have not supported his statement. Similarly, the delay in making the statement cannot be the sole ground to disbelieve the statement at this stage, especially in view of his explanation that as an Intelligence Officer, who was privy to a lot of sensitive information, he would make a statement only when he was under a legal obligation to do so".

The *amicus curiae* further said, it is quite possible that Mr Bhatt was directed to attend the meeting on 27.02.2002 at the residence of the Chief Minister. "The phone call records do not contradict the statement given by Bhatt to the SIT. Considering the important and emergent nature of the meeting, the relative "juniority" of Bhatt need not have come in the way of his attending the meeting, especially since the ADGP (Intelligence), Mr Raiger was not available". Ramachandran also said, it is anybody's guess as to why, in the absence of Mr Raiger, Mr OP Mathur [IGP (Security and Administration)], who was next in seniority, was not called for the meeting. This aspect, in my view, is of little significance in the context of an emergency meeting called at short notice in response to an escalating situation".

The *amicus curiae* report that police officer Bhatt's statement that Modi had ordered revenge against Muslims was made probable by the presence of two Ministers - Ashok Bhatt and IK Jadeja in the Ahmedabad Police Control Room at the time Muslims were being attacked. The state government's initial and weak plea was that these two ministers were only felicitating security arrangements as the then Defence Minister George Fernandes was to visit Ahmedabad the next day.

But Jaynarayan Vyas, the cabinet spokesman for Modi government, has justified the police actions against Bhatt including the arrest. "Bhatt was arrested on the basis of a police complaint filed by his own former subordinate in his private capacity", Vyas said, as per a report at *India-Behind the Lens* on 5 October, 2011.

Calling Bhatt 'a police officer with several criminal charges' since he joined in 1988, the minister said, "There were cases registered against him even before 2001 when there was no Modi government. And yet the prejudiced Congress continues to link his arrest to the Chief Minister, exposing its intention to malign the state government".

Meanwhile, in a story (1 October 2011), website *First post* reported that Bhatt's wife Shweta said she feared for her husband's life and wrote to the Ahmedabad Commissioner of Police demanding justice. "Since yesterday, I am not allowed to meet Sanjiv. The police officials are not even allowing the lawyer to meet him. Then how can we file his bail application", she said.

Shweta also wrote to Union Home Minister P Chidambaram appealing to him for Bhatt's safety and has accused the government and the state police of colluding in targeting Bhatt. Upon receiving Shweta's letter, Home Secretary RK Singh convened a high-level meeting.

"The Home Ministry has written to the Gujarat government to ensure adequate security to Bhatt and his family as per local threat perception", reported *The Economic Times* quoting a Home Ministry official.

SIT reprieve for Modi

On February 9, 2012 I woke to a typical Modi-related headline. The morning papers had screaming headlines and detail stories on how Modi had earned a crucial reprieve from the Special Investigation Team (SIT). In its report submitted to a Magistrate Court in Ahmedabad in compliance with the Supreme Court directives, the SIT had said that there was "no prosecutable evidence" against Narendra Modi for abetting the 2002 communal riots. A five-member Special Investigation Team (SIT), headed by former CBI head RK Raghavan was set up by the Supreme Court in 2009. It said among other things mere inaction or negligence on the part of Modi would not invite criminal action if there was no *mens-rea* (motivated criminal intention). At the most, the SIT hinted that "one could say it was dereliction of duty by officials concerned".

The SIT also maintained that it was an 'after thought' on the part of Sanjiv Bhatt to allege that Modi had in his February 27, 2002 meeting with senior police officials had asked them to go slow on the arsonists. SIT, which had recorded Bhatt's testimony on the issue, maintained that there was no substantial corroborative evidence to back Bhatt's claim.

The media reports also claimed that according to the SIT, there was no material evidence to suggest that Modi had any criminal intention of orchestrating the riots.

Curiously on February 23, 2012, a Gujarati daily in Ahmedabad carried a news item based on Modi's testimony before the SIT. The Chief Minister was questioned on March 27-28, 2010 by the SIT officer AK Malhotra and the statement was considered 'classified'. In the statement, according to reports, Modi had denied about the "baseless allegation" that he had instructed cops to go slow on the rioters and instead had said, "on the contrary, I had given categorical and clear cut instructions to maintain peace and communal harmony at any cost".

Through as many as 71 questions, Modi was grilled about the entire gamut of the riots including the decision to shift the bodies to Ahmedabad from Godhra (train mayhem), attack on Congress MP Ehsan Jafri in Gulberg Society and the dreaded killings and arson in Naroda-Patiya localities in Ahmedabad.

On the crucial decision of shifting of the bodies from Godhra to Ahmedabad, which enraged public anguish violently, Modi had told reportedly the SIT that it was a "collective decision" of top police and administrative officials posted in Godhra. It was only to defuse "building up of tension in Godhra".

In March 2012, Modi, country's best known headline hunter, again made news. The popular *Time* magazine, in its March 26 issue, published an article on Modi, with the heading: "Modi means business", along with a strap: "But can he lead India?"

Congress leaders on their part thought much of that cover story on the much vilified Gujarat Chief Minister was uncalled for. "I am deeply distressed by two recent articles on Gujarat Chief Minister Narendra Modi. One is by *Time magazine* and the other is by Brookings Institution. Journalism or reporting is supposed to be balanced and impartial. I am surprised why only those, who have praised Modi, have been quoted", the Leader of the Opposition in Gujarat assembly Shaktisinh Gohil said.

Brookings Institution also had published an interview of Modi, praising him for the work done by his government for the development of Gujarat.

"These articles are an injustice to Gujarat and India, because they are biased, partial and highlight wrong facts about Gujarat", Mr Gohil said adding all those with values, all those who respect Gujarat for it is this land that gave birth to Gandhi and Sardar Patel need to protest against it strongly. "Modi thinks that by repeating a lie, it becomes the truth. Modi's Goebellian propaganda is once again reflected through these articles", Gohil had alleged.

To be precise, these articles do not say anything new or unusual. But it really remains to be understood why Congress leaders should take offence to media articles. For example, the article by Brookings Institution also says the obvious: "Modi may be branded by the riots, but what he really wanted to talk about was Gujarat's economic miracle. Gujarat's economic performance is without peer in India, growing an average 10 per cent each year for a decade. That is faster growth than almost any place on earth, including most of China. Some argue that this might have happened regardless of Modi, but what is clear is that on most key policy matters, he has defied the logic and design of Delhi policy-making".

Well, politics is also the art of inherent rivalry if not jealousy! Gohil, unlike his characteristic, sounds too personal when he says, "The article says: Gujarat has progressed like never before in Modi regime and is now most industrialised state of India. Right now, Gujarat's growth rate is about 12 per cent. Now, in 1992-93, please remember there was no liberalisation and economic reforms and at that point of time, Gujarat's growth rate was 16.75 per cent.

"Modi alone has been taking credit for Gujarat and its growth when Gujarat has traditionally been the growth centre of the nation. The *Time* or Brookings should have mentioned that", Gohil said.

In a personal attack on Modi, Gohil said, "The *Time* article, of course, has some correct facts and I have to acknowledge and congratulate the magazine for at least acknowledging that Narendra Modi is a married man, because, to begin with, his long strings of lies, masks and manipulation, Modi has never ever acknowledged his marriage".

"Modi's career began with a lie. For as we are told, the RSS constitution clearly says that their full-time pracharaks have to be unmarried, bachelors, who can devote their life to RSS. Modi began as a RSS pracharak. And so far, has never acknowledged his marriage", Mr Gohil said. The *Time* article pays tribute to Modi era in Gujarat saying, "What's certain is that during his 10 years in power in Gujarat, the state has become India's most industrialized and business-friendly territory, having largely escaped the land conflicts and petty corruption that often paralyze growth elsewhere in the nation".

"Gujarat's $85 billion economy may not be the largest in India, but it has prospered without the benefit of natural resources, fertile farmland, big population center like Mumbai or a lucrative high-tech hub like Bangalore. Gujarat's success, even Modi's detractors acknowledge, is a result of good planning – exactly what so much of India lacks.

"His **ability to get things done** is in stark contrast to the Congress-led Central Government in New Delhi".

Lokayukta Appointment dispute

The fierce legal and political battle over Lokayukta appointment issue is another important issue vis-à-vis the functioning of Narendra Modi.

His government has been reprimanded harshly by a Gujarat High Court judge who ruled against Modi government over the appointment of Gujarat's Lokayukta or ombudsman. Justice VM Sahai said, "The Chief Minister acted under a false impression that he could turn down the superiority and primacy of the opinion of the Chief Justice which was binding. The spiteful and challenging action demonstrates the false sense of invincibility".

The root of the problem remains in the unprecedented move wherein Gujarat Governor Kamla Beniwal on August 25, 2011 had appointed retired judge Justice RA Mehta as the state Lokayukta bypassing the state government, which had then challenged the decision in the High Court.

The appointment of the Lokayukta had become a contentious issue for the last seven years with Opposition Congress and ruling BJP blaming each other for the delay. "Although it is true that generally the Governor acts as per the aid and advice of the Council of Ministers headed by the Chief Minister, there might be a circumstance, where Governor could not remain mute spectator to the happenings in the state and is compelled to use discretion", a statement from the Governor's office had said.

"So...as per the provisions of Section 3(1) of the Gujarat Lokayukta Act 1986, Dr Shrimati Kamla Beniwal had used her power on August 25th and issued a warrant of appointing retired Justice RA Mehta as the Lokayukta of the state in overall interest of transparency and good governance", it added.

In a scathing attack on the Modi government for non-appointment of Lokayukta for the last seven years, the Governor further said, "Despite several reminders... for the reason best known to it, the government was delaying the matter for one reason or other". The state government had, however, challenged the Governor's order terming the decision "unconstitutional and unilateral".

On January 18, 2012, reacting to the Gujarat High Court order on Lokayukta, the Congress claimed that the verdict was another judicial confirmation of Modi's "hypocrisy" and the "double standards" of BJP.

On October 11, 2011, a Division Bench of Gujarat High Court had given a split verdict on the appointment of Lokayukta by the Governor. While Justice Kureshi had upheld the decision of Governor, Justice Gokani had quashed the Warrant of appointment issued by the Governor terming it unconstitutional. Justice VM Sahai was given the task of hearing the petition challenging the appointment of Lokayukta following the split verdict by the Division Bench.

However, wasting no time, the Gujarat government next day, January 19, moved the Supreme Court challenging the state High Court verdict upholding appointment of Justice RA Mehta as Lokayukta by Governor Kamla Beniwal. In its petition, the Gujarat government contended that the Governor's decision to appointment Mehta as Lokayukta bypassed constraints and restraints imposed by the Constitution on the Governor's office.

The divided judgment of the Gujarat High Court is a setback to federalism. The Governor is a nominee of Central Government, the Modi regime contended.

The administrative as well as politico-legal battle on Gujarat does not seem to calm down. On March 10, 2012, the controversial and suspended IPS officer Sanjiv Bhatt said that Nanavati Commission enquiring into the 2002 Gujarat riots should submit its second report to the Governor of Gujarat, and not to the state Chief Minister Narendra Modi whose role is covered by the terms of reference of the enquiry.

In a letter written to the Commission, Bhatt also demanded that even the first report of the Commission submitted to the state government should be recalled and handed over to the Gujarat Governor.

"In consonance with principle of natural justice that no person shall be a judge in his own cause, the yet-to-be submitted second report of the Commission may also be presented to the Governor and not to the Chief Minister", he said. The first report of the Commission was submitted to the Chief Minister Narendra Modi himself in September

2008, despite the fact that his role was very much the subject matter of the terms of references being enquired into by the Commission, Bhatt observed.

In the first report which covered the Godhra train burning incident, the Commission had said that it was a pre-planned conspiracy. Bhatt also pleaded with the Commission to summon Modi for deposition and cross-examination 'as the conclusion of Commission that no material was available against him was premature'. The show or politico-legal battle is still going on.

On April 22, 2012, two days after the Supreme Court stayed the proceedings against Bhatt on the custodial death, another case of custodial torture was registered against the suspended IPS officer. The new complaint was filed after directions from the Chief Judicial Magistrate MD Kundaliya at Jamnagar following a petition by a victim Vijaysinh Bhatti. The new case was in connection with an incident in 1990, in which a person allegedly suffered kidney failure after he was beaten up in the police custody.

Chapter – 6

Conclusion

Future Tense

In 2002, during the turbulent period there used to be a joke often shared in Ahmedabad that while one train compartment incident had given Gujarat its Mohandas Gandhi, another train compartment incident at Godhra (in 2002) has given the state its Narendra Modi. The comparison between the two sons of Gujarat is definitely paradoxical as both resemble two diametrically opposite sets of socio-political ideologies. As probably people of Gujarat are torn apart between these two ideologies and thought process; the state is today torn apart between its past and future.

The present is, of course, Narendra Modi. However, on his part, Modi claims Mahatma Gandhi remains a life long inspiration for him and many visitors to his office including those from abroad often say that they have been gifted among other things, with a copy of Gandhiji's autobiography.

Years back when Modi was first sworn-in as the Gujarat Chief Minister on October 7, 2001 replacing an embattled party old-war horse Keshubhai Patel, there was a small piece of story ran by PTI wire service. It spoke about Modi's swearing-in being covered live by his personal website. The IT knowledge of Indians was not yet to the mark as it is now. I was temporarily stationed at PTI's Chandigarh office for a short while. In fact, the moment the news story about website reached our desk at Chandigarh there was a brief debate on the merits of such a news report. Little wonder, Modi had kept himself low-profile but his incisive knowledge and more importantly the use of internet technology was perhaps second to none. In later years too, this interest only sustained. It would not be out of place to mention that the 'computer-mediated communication' or the internet has a profound impact on his life and career and he is using it both as a tool to promote one's personal image and also as a key system for governance. I often tell friends that had not the train inferno taken place; the little known township of Godhra had the potential of making news in IT revolution.

For Godhra and its Panchmahal district, the irony was more. On February 27, 2002 when unscrupulous elements set fire on Sabarmati Express, they not only precipitated an unprecedented communal riots in Gujarat, but the mayhem also derailed Panchmahal district from its track of long journey for IT revolution.

For Godhra and Panchmahal district; there was certainly a setback due to the violence, subsequent tension and days of curfew. On December 31, 2001, Panchmahal district and its headquarter Godhra clicked into a web history in western India when citizens in the district were given the opportunity to simply walk into a nearest STD and cyber kiosk and obtain ration cards or file pension claims. The entire credit for IT revolution cannot obviously be given to Modi alone because the process for the same had begun long back. With traders' friendly atmosphere and pragmatic business acumen of locals, Gujarat had attained e-governance network spread over to the taluka level – as against even 'CEO' N Chandrababu Naidu's Andhra Pradesh having up to district level only. That was in 2002. By now Gujarat had attained the largest number of Internet Service Providers

(30) and also emerged as a hub of four gateways and nearly 65,000 internet subscribers.

This is one part of the story of IT in Gujarat. The other part belongs to Modi. The Gujarat watchers know it pretty well that no other Chief Minister has been able to make use of IT and importantly its huge reach to his advantage and image build up.

Today, more than one newsletter regarding the state are web posted to millions of IT/email users across the globe. And I would have no hesitation that the perceptible change in people's perception about him and especially his developmental activities reach internet users - his friends and foes alike.

As I interacted over the matter with Gujarat government officials over the months, many endorsed my views rather strongly that Modi understands it pretty well that internet mediated communications/newsletters/video footage can have "transformative impact" on people's mind as more and more people are slowly getting affected by this technology. Modi is among the first group of Indian politicians making use of the technology and even social networking sites like twitter and Facebook. He has a huge following to his twitter account. Importantly, he keeps himself updated and would not miss opportunities to pass on his comments and catchy one-liners on news and events promptly.

The Gujarat watchers admit that he has also benefited by the IT and these social networking sites and newsletters. "One likes it or not, the internet has dramatically influenced his friends and foes alike. To those who view things with jaundiced eyes of a Hindu chauvinism, his twitter messages etc tell them how Hindus have been endangered. Yet again, for others, these make significant differences in changing their opinion about Modi", said a minority community public sector employee posted in Ahmedabad.

Not entirely to my surprise, he further told me that as elsewhere jihadi networks or closer home, how Anna Hazare's crusade, have used internet as logistical and publicity tool; Modi is one of the rare Indian politicians who has been using this too. Adept application of the net especially in terms of making use of the free web space have gone to his advantage to manipulate public opinion and as well as the press agendas.

Modi has understood it pretty well that a website's greatest contribution is to remove the prospect of compartmentalizing an event, any propaganda or a theory. It is this so-called worldview – actually rightly influenced by his propaganda – that has fetched him dividends in terms of investors making a beeline for his state.

It is a known fact, both old and new, and even corporate sector endorses that effective publicity does help bring in new players. Therefore, it is not quite surprising that when Maruti Suzuki had to shift its unit from strike-torn Haryana, the choice was Gujarat. When Ratan Tata was turned away from Bengal, he also called up Modi and when Delhi Metro compartment-maker Canadian firm, Bombardier had to look for a place in India, the natural choice was Modi's Gujarat.

In other words, Modi's image is being rechristened or reshaped by the internet as the web technology is definitely having an increasing impact on his voters in Gujarat, Indian citizens in general and rest of the world in varied and diverse contemporary contexts.

The best eulogizing of Modi's developmental works would be summed up in the saying that in today's world, it is not merely resources that lead one to take a decision rather it is the decision that makes the resources.

According to his admirers the best gift of Modi as the chief executive of the state has been to lead his government and bureaucracy to take necessary decisions quickly. According to the article run by Brookings Institution, Modi has also taken up with the Prime Minister Manmohan Singh, asking whether the states can have their own representatives at key embassies overseas to generate funds. He expressed great interest in the fact that American states often have their own offices, independent of US embassies. Creditably for Modi, not many chief ministers either in the past or at present have thought on these lines.

William Antholis, managing director of the Brookings Institution and a senior fellow in Governance Studies, perhaps rightly summed up his opinion on Modi: "I came away thinking that this was a man America needed to know better. He may never be able to move past his role in the 2002 riots. But he is a talented and effective political leader, and will continue pushing New Delhi and not following. He has successfully tackled some of India's toughest problems, but also has touched its most sensitive nerves. One thing is certain— he will continue to be a force in Indian politics".

Corporate executives, though, tend to concentrate on Modi's pro-business attributes, which they see as something of a 'pleasant exception' in India where bureaucracy, red-tapism and corruption do hinder works.

Here I will present a case of red-tapism of babus in one-time red-flagged Left ruled state of West Bengal, and now under their Communists' worst known *bête noire* of all time Mamata Banerjee.

This relates to the flagship rural job scheme Mahatma Gandhi National Rural Employment Guarantee Act (MG-NREGA).

In October 2011, the West Bengal rural development and panchayats secretary Barun Roy was reprimanded by the Central Government for allegedly rejecting a proposal of the East Midnapore MG-NREGA committee, which is headed by the Union Minister of State for Rural Development, Sishir Adhikari. At the committee's 29th June 2011 meeting under the chairmanship of Adhikari, a key Trinamool leader, proposals were passed for implementing concrete road, *pucca* drain and concrete ground wall for creating durable assets.

However, in his August 17th (2011) missive to the district magistrate, he rejected the proposals (obviously sitting in his Kolkata office) saying these were in direct contravention of 'operational guidelines for MG-NREGA'.

The *babudom* argument of Barun Roy was that 'durable projects' could not be taken up as there is no mention about the same in the NREGA guidelines. Now in several states there has been no such major hurdle either from the babus or other authorities in the state governments. In fact, states like Andhra Pradesh, Assam and Maharashtra have shown flexibility and taken up such *pucca* roads and other durable projects. According to Adhikari, it is such *babudom* which has resulted in poor utilization of funds in states like West Bengal.

After 2007 assembly polls in particular, Modi dedicated himself solely to the goal of changing his image to a pro-development man. The efforts brought in dividends too. In circa 2011, Gujarat has managed a turnaround and achieved 11 per cent agricultural growth, despite its fast track industrial development. His rivals do not want to credit Modi and term these as mere 'process of survival and high talent for Gujarati entrepreneurship', but the march towards progress in the field of agriculture, infrastructural facilities like drinking water, education, employment, transportation, manufacturing and tourism is worth lauding. In terms of statistics, even in agricultural growth while the national growth rate is around three per cent; Gujarat has crossed the double digit figure of nearly eleven per cent.

Though both urban and rural living conditions have improved in Gujarat, especially over the last 10 years, it's only natural that this has happened unevenly. At the end of the day, shedding all hypes about Gujarat development, it ought to be stated that Modi and his government derived the legitimacy to govern the state in the eyes of the common people not by pure issue of effective governance or even democratic methodology, but by repeated reference to a unique synthesis of parochial Gujarati pride and the chauvinism of Hindutva. Thus, Gujarat's developmental journey too cannot be divorced from the overall character of developmental phenomenon in the modern times – that it means well-being, profits and luxury of already the rich and not so much transition in poor and so-called *'aam admi's'* life. If the oft-repeated argument from the centre, that price hike of essential commodities also has to do with the state's role, it is curious to look at ways and means adopted by the Modi regime in last so many months to give succor to the poorer lot.

A 2010 report by a US-based research organization puts Gujarat among the five worst performing states in India in reducing hunger, along with Bihar, Madhya Pradesh, Chhattisgarh and Jharkhand. Another survey claimed that in worker' wage share, Gujarat has fallen from 23 to 8 per cent. So, who is really seeing the development in Gujarat?

Modi's former Home Minister and now a critic Zadafia says, "Gujarat development is for Ambanis and the likes". The gap between incomes of the rich and the poor has risen to more than the national average, says a 2010 paper by Rajesh Shukla of the National Council of Applied Economics Research. But this throws a follow-up question at the same time: If Gujarat is one of the lowest performers in terms of social equity despite the growth graph, which other state in India can match it? Has economic development since 1991 helped social equity uplift in any other state?

Narendra Modi and the BJP would do well to see certain basic facets of socio-political existence vis-à-vis development. Gujarat still remains a much law abiding state in general sense despite the much slammed history of communal chauvinism.

A typical characteristic of Hindu chauvinism is that the law of the land holds no terror for the law breakers – once they can justify it with religious colour. As a result, a vice like corruption is bound to crop up even if the fear of Modi is keeping things under the carpet. Popular writer Trevor Fishlock was right when he wrote long back that corruption has many roots --- greed, need and cynicism among them. In the context of Gujarat too, one need not work very hard to find these factors.

Like elsewhere, anyone would like to prosper and even the participation of the middle class in 2002 looting spree can be attributed to these baser instincts. People generally give priority to self and family over the broader interests of making contributions and ensuring corruption-free working of the state and civil machineries.

No one is, however, a sacred cow here. Needless to add, people in Gujarat are as prone to greed and as needy to materialistic consumerism as elsewhere if not more, as most other citizens across the country. Corruption is here to stay. Even if it is deplored in one voice; yet there are behind the screen players albeit in microscopic numbers endorsing it. Congress leaders already draw a parallel between the Gujarat Chief Minister and the former Karnataka chief minister, BS Yeddyurappa, who even spent days cooling heels behind bars.

True, for politicians corruption menace is essentially a hot potato revolving mostly around the approach line of holier than thou. Modi camp is blowing its own trumpet around the slogan that "*na hum khate haein. Na khane deten haein* (we are neither corrupt nor we will allow corruption)".

At the same time, middle-level entrepreneurs and others say government servants still know the tricks and often found conniving with unscrupulous elements making fortunes by indulging in financial defalcation. They cite the instances that despite much claim about probity in public life under Modi and to a large extent true; there are cases when government officials and neo-politicians often throw lavish banquets and move around in costly vehicles, the poor villagers have to beg and borrow to raise the required 'bribe' to get their work done. Such instances also lead to negligence and indifference of government apparatus towards their responsibilities.

In the case of agricultural works too, the state cannot be indifferent. As underlined earlier, large scale focus on industrialization has affected the agri sector.

The ideological statement that agriculture is the best means of man's livelihood has fallen flat in today's Gujarat, wherein the Chief Minister is in a tiring hurry to enhance his image by pushing industries and facilitating easy and smooth grazing for industries especially the large houses, both from within the country and abroad.

Today, it is a reality that modern bookish education and industrialization punctuated with craze for white collar jobs and the call centre culture backed by fatter pay-packets have taken the people off the fields. Moreover, as strongly argued by the Union Agriculture Minister, Sharad Pawar, the successful implementation of UPA's flagship scheme like MG-NREGA has enhanced the purchasing power of rural labour class too. Sociologists believe that if education spreads unemployment and dependency, it is far dangerous than ignorance and illiteracy. These challenges ought to be looked into minutely.

The Gujarat government insiders maintain that while the overall incidences of crime in Gujarat stood lower compared to other states but in crimes against women and juveniles it is considerably high. The total number of crimes against women in Gujarat in 2010 was recorded at 8,616 though it stood much less than states like Andhra Pradesh, which had topped the list with 24,111 cases, followed by Uttar Pradesh 23,569 and West Bengal 20,912 cases.

In some parts of the country, say for example West Bengal, Chhattisgarh, Jharkhand, Andhra Pradesh and Odhisa, people already know about the menace of Naxalism. Thus, the state of Gujarat will do well to appreciate fully well that confronted with hard realities of economic life and social indifference as is with the Muslims, how much harm can be done by compartmentalizing the state into industrially (or entrepreneurship) haves and have-nots. Otherwise, the state should be ready to face a situation where its people can be crippled. These vices can blind the vision and destroy the will of a community which is otherwise determined to triumph, perhaps with Modi and also without him.

According to a report in *The Indian Express*, state Directorate of Economics and Statistics, Gandhinagar, compiled figure for 'Gujarat among the States of India 2010' and the cold statistics speak for themselves.

It says while Modi's Gujarat is the second most industrialized state in India after Maharashtra and figures in the top 10 in terms of economic indicators such as GDP and Net State Domestic Product (NSDP), the performance has been less impressive in terms of social indicators like education and health. What would never do Narendra Modi proud is that in some yardsticks Gujarat's performance is even worse than the national averages.

In health, the malnutrition level for children below five years (45 per cent) is higher than the national average (43 per cent). There have been more malnourished children under five in Gujarat than in many large states like Tamil Nadu (30 per cent), Maharashtra (37 per cent), Rajasthan (40 per cent), Odisha (41 per cent) and Uttar Pradesh (42 per cent).

According to the 2008 statistics from the union Ministry of Home Affairs, Gujarat's infant mortality rate was higher than Kerala, Tamil Nadu, Punjab, Karnataka and even Naxal-hit Jharkhand.

According to the 2007-08 figures of the Union Ministry of Human Resource Development (HRD), the drop out rate in Gujarat in classes I to X is 57.5 per cent for boys (against the national average of 56.4) and 61.2 for girls (against the national average of 57.3). However, the Gujarat government has undertaken several steps and had brought in the improvement.

As many as 1,23,808 cases of cognizable crimes were registered in Gujarat in 2008. This includes 1,106 cases of murder and 1,809 cases of clash. Another 20,715 cases of theft, 5,053 of burglary and 1,322 of robbery were also recorded. Nationally, Madhya Pradesh (MP) topped the list with the highest numbers of cognizable offences followed by Maharashtra (2,06,243) and Karnataka (1,27,540), Bihar followed Gujarat with 1,22,669 cases. The lowest was recorded in Sikkim (730 cognizable offences).

The overall incidences of crime in Gujarat may be lower compared to other states but in crimes against women and juveniles it is considerably high. The total number of crimes against women in Gujarat was recorded at 8,616. Andhra Pradesh topped the list with 24,111 cases, followed by Uttar Pradesh (23,569) and West Bengal (20,912) cases. In Gujarat, 374 cases of rape and 828 of molestation were recorded.

The number of domestic violence cases, especially cruelty from husband and relatives was high (6,094). The cases of juvenile crime in Gujarat were recorded at 1,074. The highest number of juvenile crime cases was found in MP (4,259) followed by UP (4,078) and Maharashtra (2,709).

Adaptability breakdown

Gujarat is today developing and it is happening rather fast. But in the craze of these developments, many fear the state is perhaps having some kind of 'adaptability breakdown'. Modi is only fanning that ego and in the process other aspects of life are afraid to be put into second fiddle. To analyze the result of such a scenario, one need not struggle much. Today's angry streets in America and Europe are only testimony of the gross failure of such insane materialistic development.

An insider in Modi camp mailed me certain statistics arguing eloquently that had Gujarat been a nation of its own, it would be 67th richest nation in the world above many European and Asian economies like China and Ukraine.

- Gujarat holds many records in India for economic development:

- 20 per cent of India's Industrial Output
- 9 per cent of India's Mineral Production
- 22 per cent of India's exports
- 24 per cent of India's textile production
- 35 per cent of India's pharmaceutical products
- 51 per cent of India's petro-chemical production

Gujarat ranks top nationwide in gas-based thermal electricity generation with national market share of over 8 per cent.

Over 35 per cent of the stock market wealth of India is with Gujarati people.

About 60 per cent of Indian population in North America is Gujarati.

Even the first VEG Pizaa Hut was opened in Ahmedabad.

Surat is the fastest growing city in the world, while Ahmedabad is the 7th largest city in India. Gandhinagar is the Greenest Capital City in whole Asia.

Ahmedabad is ranked 2nd in Real Estate – Ahead of Bangalore, Chennai, Hyderabad, Mumbai and Delhi.

Now, the pro-Modi camp is dismissive of the charge of saffronization of the administration, something that cannot be denied for obvious reasons though. But it is also true that much current thinking, media mud-slinging and blistering attack on Modi is the product of stereo-type text book or television view knowledge.

The Indian development is a reality at least in the regional canvas and more in the context of the regional forum of BRICS.

Gujarat in more ways than one reflects that story of multi-pronged development. Many are already comparing Gujarat's phenomenal success with the select manufacturing hub of China; but the irony is not lost on many.

Although, the Indian development pace is much slower than China's; even in late nineties Gujarat had equalled the growth rate of China.

The developmental phases of Modiland notwithstanding the negative publicity of the state administration since 2002 have many people baffled. There are a few questions too --- can Modi really redefine the State's and more importantly his own reputation?

Can it keep the balance with the traditional culture of Gujarat, its religious bias and the unprecedented benefits of economic liberalization?

Now, let us try to take the debate on development and social sectors yardsticks into a different plane.

Firstly, India's reforms have come in compartmentalized forms. In the absence of reforms in the administration, police and judiciary, the new rules were enforced by an old system, and the mismatch has led to weak enforcement. The competition in presence of multiple players say in telecom could overcome weak enforcement. This appears to be a factor responsible for the success of equity markets and telecom but the same story was not reaped in the oil and power sectors.

Many would argue that in a complex society like ours and in multi-layered polity of democracy in India, the consensual process of reform is important for success. There is no doubt in the last two decades that the policy-makers, the ministers and the law-makers either in state assemblies or in Parliament, have spent time listening to groups, business chambers etc before embarking on major policy changes. So did even a supposed autocrat Modi. But his success story also underlines that 'out of the box' thinking is highly advisable. Here was a chief minister, who despite the bad press, to the industry has always remained a 'vanguard' of not only change but someone who stood for what he said. Mere mechanical imitation of best practices often fails.

When Modi invited Ratan Tata after the latter's Bengal misadventure, at least the corporate honcho knew that Gujarat would welcome his project. Therefore, Ratan Tata chose Gujarat for his Nano. A good and concrete solution possibly in a short span of time is always one that has worked in Gujarat's favour; and this calls for some credit for the state Chief Minister.

A senior socialist based in Faizabad in UP, I interacted within course of my work on the book, actually said something sensational putting me into a track to ponder about his point of argument. He said Modi should be considered as an "injured tiger" - caged and pushed to the wall by constant vilification. The blot of 2002 had created a sort of a crisis for him. Fortunately, for Modi, said my friend, he had no choice but to prove his responsibility in administration and that too for development.

Were it not for Modi having to confront a full-scale war against him by the rival politicians and the secular brigade, it is unlikely that Modi would have pushed his developmental card so hard and decisively. Maybe, maybe not!

The socialist leader claiming to know Modi personally, maintained that before being elevated as the Chief Minister, Modi was a typical lower runged BJP *neta* and was always overshadowed by the galaxy of media savvy players like Pramod Mahajan, Sushma Swaraj and Govindacharya.

"But today things have gone in Modi's favour. He might be a Muslim-baiter; but today he has brought in sustained acceleration in growth, perceptible progress against otherwise awful toll of poverty and the image of non-performing *netas*", he said.

According to him, Moditva today as if a case of the 'caged and injured tiger' was waiting to be truly set free.

Look at the results: the same Chief Minister vilified in the nation and who was denied a US visa in 2005 is wooed by corporate of all hues. He is finding himself engaged with top industrialists within the country and overseas and also there is engagement with the global economic power like China.

His admirers have reasons therefore when they say Narendra Modi has changed the rules of Indian politics to an extent as from Nitish Kumar to Mamata Banerjee -- everybody is following his footsteps by organizing business summits and instead of rushing to Delhi with begging bowls are trying out to look for investment in their respective states based on their own strengths. The alleged ill-treatment meted out to non-Congress state governments by the Centre today has provoked angry comments from

Modi and even the likes of Jayalalithaa, Naveen Patnaik and importantly, UPA constituent, Mamata Banerjee-led Trinamool Congress.

Modi has also set the pace for inclusive growth, something cherished and given a lip-service in most cases. There is no denying that at the national level too, despite having someone like Manmohan Singh at the helm; too much of growth has been concentrated in a narrow part of the economy - IT, BPO and some urban-based sectors. But in Modi's Gujarat, there have been actions of the ground for generating mass employment with focused approach for expansion in manufacturing. The Gujarat government, despite its lapses, has also taken steps for high-value agriculture and food processing.

Therefore, what can be the measure of Modi's success rate on the developmental front? He has put the subject of rebalancing the growth chart on the agenda. The question in Gujarat and in those minds interested in Gujarat affairs is: whether his developmental saga has to be checked or reversed? On the contrary, the clamour is for taking these to the newer heights, as a key minister in the Modi cabinet summed up.

When it comes to analyzing the success tales of Modi in the last decade, perhaps it is only natural to try to understand how the Chief Minister's popularity has grown.

In all realms of governance and socio-political epitaph today, Gujarat's story is the story of Narendra Modi. It is a replica of Jayalalithaa culture and a unique synthesis of the same style one had in Andhra Pradesh under Chandrababu Naidu or Jyoti Basu in Bengal.

Like the Leftists, BJP too is a cadre-based party but it is not the party machineries but what matters significantly is what the chief minister is saying or doing. True, these are nothing new, but yet there are a few stark exceptions too. From the die-hard anti-Musharraf rhetoric to sarcastic remarks on Muslim society allowing men to keep four wives – *'hum panch hamare pachis'* – Modi has lately turned to newer horizon.

From what was Gujarat largely known as a Hindutva laboratory, he has now thrown in a challenge that his state should be seen as a 'development model'. His fan following in the state is not complaining yet. Even central ministers under Manmohan Singh in Delhi believe that Modi's popularity is reaching new heights not because of Hindutva slogans or anything else but for his developmental works.

However, there is yet another version on this. A large number of his detractors like Congress leader Shaktisinh Gohil and former state MoS Home, Gordhan Zadafia have said that Modi is running an autocracy in the state. His ministers often are caught unawares of developmental schemes announced under their responsibilities; while the bureaucracy is more or less in a "state of suspended animation".

Zadafia spoke to me at length and made certain remarks.

"So much is the awe about Moditva that no single civil servant in his senses had dared cross the path of the Chief Minister," Zadafia said.

According to Modi detractors, the wings of the bureaucracy have been clipped over the years or made 'saffronized' or rather tailored to make them subservient to the whims of one man – the Chief Minister.

A number of pliable officers have thrived including the former Ahmedabad Police Commissioner PC Pandey; while others like Sanjiv Bhatt and even their families are suffering.

The CAG reports on Gujarat talk about defalcation to the tune of Rs 26, 652 crore, according to Congress leaders. The CAG report of 2008-09 said that the state government's compliance with various rules, procedures and directives was unsatisfactory, which was evident from the delays in furnishing utilization certificates against the loans and grants received from various grantee institutions.

The government reported 178 cases of misappropriation, defalcation, etc., involving Government money amounting to Rs 8.73 crore up to March 2009, the CAG had said adding the internal controls in all the organizations should be strengthened to prevent such cases in future. But for the Modi government CAG reports have remained a contentious issue which propelled it on defensive. In Gandhinagar, the Gujarat government believes that the observations made in the Comptroller and Auditor General (CAG) reports cannot be considered a final proof of a particular department or officials heading it being corrupt. It called CAG reports placed in the state assembly as "merely preliminary observations". But in the same breath at the national level, the BJP does not miss a minute to mount attack on the UPA and Congress for alleged corruption allegations in CAG report on Commonwealth Games against the PMO and the Delhi Chief Minister.

Shaktisinh Gohil, Congress leader and Opposition leader in Gujarat assembly, even mocks at Modi's China trip in 2011. "Gujarat Chief Minister Narendra Modi visited China to learn how to copy and deliver cheap things to people, the art which is mastered by China", he had said at Gujarat Congress's Jan Adhikar Sammelan in Mahesana.

Till far, as one comes to the concluding phase of the last chapter, this book has failed those who want to know, what really sparked off the inferno at Godhra railway station on February 27, 2002. This book has not told either, whether Modi will come out unscathed in the series of trials of cases related to the Gujarat riots or that he would end up facing chargesheet or will one day address from the ramparts of the Red Fort in near future.

Modi's conflicting images have so far made things interesting as well as curious. But it ought to be stated that his Hindutva zealot image is working as a RSS favourite – which might not be entirely true. On the other hand, Modi's apparent journey – stealing all the limelight for Gujarat's developments single-handedly has led to hostile whispering against him in the party. No second generation BJP leaders, the likes of Sushma Swaraj and Arun Jaitley are keen to give him the space for the prime minister's job, although Jaitley is a Rajya Sabha member from Gujarat.

Like all human beings, Modi too has weakness and ambition. One serious point due to these two combined factors is his inability to share the power and glory. He has rivals within the Sangh and BJP and all types of enemies outside – like a group of former and serving cops, the rival Congress politicians and the indifferent Congress-led UPA regime in Delhi. He is just not acceptable to NDA especially the flamboyant Nitish Kumar-Sharad Yadav led Janata Dal (United).

Till his name is cleared off all charges for the 2002 riots and other high-profile cases like Ehsan Jafri, Ishrat Jahan, Sohrabuddin and Sanjiv Bhatt and several others, it would be extremely difficult for Modi to find himself acceptable to pan-India voters. BJP too could find it near impossible to prop him as their prime ministerial candidate. The BJP leaders may not admit; and even if a few of them do that – they are in extremely microscopic minority. One direct consequence of Modi's role in the riots and the BJP leaders' failure to live up to the people's expectations in several states – is a great deal of cynicism about what BJP leaders and their governments can deliver.

The popular unpopularity BJP attained for them in Karnataka due to corruption is a glaring example – which simply takes off all the sheen of BJP's anti-corruption fight against the Congress-led UPA.

It's not a novice practicing politician in Dr Manmohan Singh, when he says; BJP too has 'skeletons' in its cupboard.

In 2012, BJP was put on extreme defensive after an element within the party pushed for a character called Anshuman Mishra for Rajya Sabha from Jharkhand. At the meeting of the parliamentary party in New Delhi on March

20, 2012, Yashwant Sinha, former finance minister and a party veteran from Jharkhand, said, "our MLAs should not be put on the auction block to the highest bidder". This gave a chance to BJP's rivals to take a potshot at the saffron party, which never hesitates to claim being an outfit with a difference. Gurudas Dasgupta, CPI floor leader, in Lok Sabha said, "There is a gap between the cup and the lip" and said the episode brought to the fore the double standards of the party.

Despite the attempt to interpret a recent Supreme Court ruling on Ehsan Jafri case as a relief and reprieve for Modi, the truth is that the apex court has only asked the trial court to decide the case and has not commented on the allegations against Modi. Therefore, the news for him is not good yet vis-à-vis these cases notwithstanding the bravado.

It's true; Gujarat has achieved multi-pronged developments in recent times. The Gujaratis have rewarded the Chief Minister Modi twice in a row. Today, Gujarat is being compared with the manufacturing hub of China. However, in the preceding pages, we have tried to establish an argument that prosperity alone does not lead to idealism of secular and pluralistic values or modernization and accommodation.

The social prosperity is seldom accompanied by the moral order. Many say the moral order as was understood traditionally and even in Gujarati folktales is increasingly vanishing under the pressure of survival and challenges associated with so-called modernization. Ace journalist Kuldip Nayar maintains that the BJP tried to project Modi on the national scene by his *Sadbhavna* Fast in September 2011, the saffron party did not attempt in any way to wash away the "bloodstains of Modi's administration". He further says, "The development work goes to his (Modi's) credit. But the Gujaratis are a gritty, hardworking community and will do in every clime", he wrote in his column 'Between the lines'. (September 22, 2011 *The Statesman*)

The core values have been vanishing fast and the former Prime Minister Atal Behari Vajpayee's appeal of 'Raj Dharma' (ethics of ideal governance) were taken casually long time back. Though Modi has tried to present his government as a clean and bereft of corruption, a few cases, as we discussed earlier, have surfaced from time to time.

But there cannot be denial about cronyism. Modi detractors including those in BJP say, as the Chief Minister gave upon him an authoritarian power; public offices have been often treated as positional goods to be distributed as rewards for loyalty. Though there is claim of quick clearance of files and less of red-tapism, no major administrative reforms have been brought in.

A bitter fact of governance everywhere is that it is the performance at the lower level that counts more. On this, it is difficult to say things have really improved.Work shirkers still rule the roost in the lower level bureaucracy, especially in the far-flung districts and in rural areas.

In fact, not only Modi, the vices like saffronization of the village home guard and state police was near complete under Modi's illustrious predecessor Keshubhai Patel.

Looking back, Gujarat's as well as India's economic journey has treaded through quite a mixed track since independence. In the initial days, C Rajagopalachari, country's first Governor General, arguably was against the permit and license raj.

For others, like Jawaharlal Nehru and even Sardar Vallabhbhai Patel, socialism and central planning was almost a fashionable attraction. Gandhi's ideas of village republics were hardly taken seriously. After 1971, Indira Gandhi backed her slogan of 'Garibi Hatao' with concrete steps like nationalizing the face of industry, like the coal industry. The formation of Coal India Limited in 1975 was a path-breaking step, but soon this organization and scores of other PSUs had turned into liabilities. In 1980, Coal India Limited had about seven lakh employees and was sustaining a loss of $ 60 million.

So today, when we talk of keeping balance with Gujarat's development, are we suggesting the need of state control in every thing that's done in the name of economic projects. Not long ago, the former Disinvestment Minister Arun Shourie had said he failed to understand the logic in government running hotels or undertaking similar works.

But the disinvestment too has its evil impact. The disinvestment of a popular hotel in Mumbai had led many workers jobless and according to former Shiv Sena-turned Congress MP, Sanjay Nirupam, some of ill-fated workers also committed suicide.

One is afraid in case of Gujarat the result would be worse as apparently all these developments are dependent primarily on one small factor called Narendra Modi. What happens when Modi is out of the scene and say, Sonia Gandhi's Congress replaces him with like a more pliable (howsoever inefficient) Shivraj Patil?

Well, if this small factor is handled well with Modi being replaced by yet another efficient chief minister; one should not lose the sight of the bigger issue. What would happen to all these developments and investment if there is another round of 2002 riots – even at much lower scale?

Another vital point that ought to be understood is that no matter how much image build up measures and web media management is resorted to by the Modi camp, it's a fact that the Gujarat Chief Minister's developmental efforts achievements since 2002-03 has only commanded little public confidence. In some quarters, they are still bitterly resisted and worse, suspected. My interactions with Congress leaders in Gujarat and some Modi baiters among intellectuals in the state only reveal the obvious that many Gujaratis seemed to have no better choice than to accept Modi's government as a *fait accompli*. This is no sign of good governance.

This section, presumably believes that Gujarat's ambitions of greater pace of development with or without Modi is comparable to a caged tiger, which is still to be released.

But in the same breath, it must be emphasized that Modi's development card coupled with a characteristic mix of Hindutva and parochial Gujarati pride have changed the rules of politics, much as some of his bitter critics would wish to deny.

One long term impact is that Modi has been able to create a legitimacy for himself in states like Tamil Nadu and Punjab as well in overseas countries including China. Along with brand Modi, there is also talk about brand Gujarat as an industrial hub. This is a great success, and one that is being followed or aped in several other states. On November 24, 2011 addressing an interactive session with industrial captains and diplomatic gathering on the theme of 'Bengal Rising: Land of Opportunities' in New Delhi, Mamata Banerjee announced launching of a business summit in January 2012 in Kolkata, the immediate comparison was with Modi's Vibrant Gujarat.

This is certainly a true measure of Modi's achievement though it cannot erase the ugly shadows of 2002 and the questionable encounters carried by his police force mostly misusing or using his name. The question, therefore is not whether Modi's developmental works have succeeded or not; but how far these were able to give him a new image.

The pro-Modi camp in BJP articulates well another vital fact that at the national level since Manmohan Singh's liberalization leap forward, the imbalance in India's development and enrichment is instantly uneven.

It's true that too much of the growth is concentrated in the realm of westernized and modern materialism like IT and BPO culture and enhanced urbanization. This has resulted in gross neglect of deeper sectors of economy, especially rural employment, infrastructure development and agriculture. This is where, they say, Modi's regime has given focused attention on manufacturing, agriculture and food processing and even high-value agriculture – which can ensure mass employment and better yields in economic terms for larger section of the population.

There is yet another facet of reforms in governance vis-à-vis socio-economic policies. Understandably, the economists and financial managers would have focused on reforms only in the context of the economic policy.

But all good governance boils down to the issue of public goods only. There needs a closer scrutiny on how law and order are the most important aspect of public goods. Here comes the role of police. It is in this context, they say Gujarat Chief Minister has asked the state home department to develop a 100-hour module in collaboration with Rakshashakti University in which each trained police officer would serve as mentor to junior colleagues and constables for 18 months.

Speaking at a passing out parade of police personnel, Modi had pointed out that the pattern of crime has undergone sea change with application of technology. Thus, he said the responsibility of uniformed men too has increased manifold with round-the-clock duty, stress and strain, and risk to life associated with the job. Hence, the need for such a module.

Like his critics and admirers admit, Modi functions like a modern day CEO laying emphasis on the outcome and often allegedly putting the rules and normal norms into backburner. If his government helped Ratan Tata in 2008, it did come to the help of other corporate players as well from Bambardier to Maruti. Such delivery level is appreciated but skeptics also wonder whether all procedures are being followed or reduced to a mere whimsical clearance by the Chief Minister just because it would go well with his image building exercises. A good-governance should also have proper checks and balances; and these are not happening.

So there are already talks about the cost of making things hassle-free for big businessmen. But, first hand accounts say even small-time entrepreneurs are benefiting by the overall atmosphere. The state government officials deny that there is any special treatment for anyone and that a clear policy driven approach make things move. Many things and essential works are done in advance through IT facilities and thus when entrepreneurs or business houses come to the government for final clearance, things move fast.

Industry players like Adi Godrej and Ratan Tata have time and again said that single party government and a decisive chief minister also contribute their part in pushing matters, unlike in a state like Maharashtra wherein the pulls from coalition partners like NCP and Congress often end up creating hassles. Even in single-party Congress-ruled Haryana and Andhra Pradesh, these are lacking because the fear of high command, some sacred cows in Delhi often prevent things moving. Industrialists admit that the cross purposes the government and the Sonia Gandhi-led UPA or even Rahul Gandhi himself often add to the administrative and business delivery woes even at the Central Government level.

Moreover, some point out that Congress has Union Ministers like Jairam Ramesh, who as in-charge of environment ministry, often blocked projects deciding by the tour programme of his 'real boss' – Rahul Gandhi. In Gujarat, to the contrary, Modi has put his party into the second fiddle and other one-time influential forces like VHP and Praveen Togadia have been forced to vanish from the scene.

Lately, even Maharashtra has lost some key business projects and investments from major players. None other than Maratha strongman Sharad Pawar attributed this to Congress-NCP 'faulty' policies. He even cited the example of Mahindra and Mahindra's decision to defer further investment in the state.

In fact, as late as 2nd June, 2012, the automobile major Maruti Suzuki India Limited (MSIL) signed a State Support Agreement (SSA) with the government of Gujarat for setting up their first Auto Vehicle manufacturing facility in Gujarat. Maruti Suzuki will set up two units in two phases in the backward Taluka of Mandal-Becharaji Amadavad district. The first unit (1st phase) will be near the historical town of Becharaji and second unit (2nd phase) will come up at a location of around 25 km from Becharaji. Notably, manufacturing and engineering sector in Gujarat contributes over 27 per cent to state GSDP and contributes overall 9 per cent to the national engineering out put.

Shinzo Nakanishi, MD, Maruti Suzuki, said the first phase of the plant is expected to be commissioned with a total anticipated investment of about Rs 4000 crore. The first phase in its full capacity will roll out 7,50,000 vehicles per year. There will be more than 2000 direct employment in each phase and more than 10000 indirect employments in each phase.

Gujarat has more than thirty engineering clusters and more are emerging in Sanand-Viramgam, Mandal-Becharaji, Halol-savli, Anjar, Santhalpur.

Gujarat is not a development-starved state like Bihar or a supposed epitome of financial mismanagement like West Bengal was under the Left for 35 long years. Gujaratis are themselves a community of immense talent for trade and entrepreneurship. It has been also a business friendly state and long before Modi had come into the scene, Ahmedabad was designated as the 'Manchester of East' as the textile hub and a trader's paradise. Modi did not have to move the sky to bring Gujarat on the development track; he has only put it on the faster rails, unlike Nitish Kumar of Bihar or Mamata Banerjee of Bengal. While Nitish inherited a Lalu legacy of whimsical administration and precarious law and order situation in Bihar, Mamata Banerjee's government says it is 'sandwiched' between the wrongdoings of the Left and the 'indifference' of the Congress-led centre.

It is economic mismanagement by the erstwhile Left regime that has put Mamata Banerjee-government into debt-trap and she is making sustained request to the centre for moratorium. Gujarat did not have these problems.

Moreover, as during my trip to a development-starved and Naxal-hit state of Jharkhand, I was told by a senior official that developments in Gujarat and that in his own state had a perceptible difference. "In Gujaratis, you have a hardworking community. Showing results in fields is in their DNA. I am afraid this is not the case in eastern India like Bihar, Bengal and my state Jharkhand", he said candidly.

"A good job in eastern India unlike a busy city like Mumbai is a job where we have 'kamai (good salary)', 'malai (extra income)' and no or less work," he added.

The real challenge in governance in Gujarat has been and still continues to be the challenge to ensure enhanced social security and communal harmony. But it goes without saying that the concept of 'social security' is not a straightjacket phenomenon as it might appear on the face value. The scale of communal problem by which an ordinary Gujarati, either Muslim or a Hindu, is threatened actually cannot be appreciated in a city like Mumbai or many other parts of the country. Here the rate of communal tensions always ranked higher.

The primary question, security for whom and from whom/what would be very interesting to answer. In Gujarat, both Hindus and the Muslims have been oppressors and the oppressed in general sense and after 2002, Modi, the state's 'chief administrator', is considered to be a party to the game. Gujarat's major problem has been its breakdown of social structures. There is absence of social leadership and unlike the past, the state has been unable to put up strong leaders. See for instance, Mahatma Gandhi, Sardar Vallabhbhai Patel and even Mohammed Ali Jinnah were from Gujarat and in later stage; it gave Morarji Desai and others. Today, the scene is different. The Congress is dreaming to oust Modi by merely playing soft Hindutva card and depending on a former BJP and RSS turncoat, Shankersinh Vaghela. The BJP also propped up leaders like Keshubhai Patel, a mofusil variety type or Suresh Mehta, whose stint as the chief minister was as ineffective as perhaps Shivraj Patil's stint as Home Minister of India.

Social security and harmony signifies a complex process which embraces key components like: Hindu-Muslim relation, Gujarati non-Gujarati relation, effective policing, speedy and fair judicial system, role of other social development indicators and the development in core sectors like employment, health and education. Having said these, one must also add that political contexts to achieve success in these elementary facets could vary from state to state. The hyped communal tension between Hindus and Muslims of Gujarat, as stated above, is never understood in a city like Mumbai or Delhi or even Kolkata. On one hand, we could stress on stereo-type phrases like holistic approach, but this might not fit Gujarat's demand.

Modi is right when he says that in a state where there have been riots over children flying kites, the corrective measures as being envisioned by the prism from Mumbai or Delhi simply might not work.

The manner in which anti-Modi campaign for the 2002 riots is largely sustained by secular brigade and NGO workers from outside Gujarat is a pointer on how Modi can still successfully get away with his 'six crore Gujarati pride' trump card. Modi's creation of a Gujarati pride is his principal asset any day, albeit he has done so by excluding Muslims and even taunting them as being pro-Miya Musharraf.

Modi played his Gujarati pride card both in 2002 and in 2007 assembly elections. When post-Godhra incident fetched him large scale criticism, he did lambast the national media and the non-Gujarati political class for insulting the people of Gujarat. "It's the same media who had described Gujaratis as 'blanket thieves", he had said. On the eve of 2002 polls, he kept harping on the point that he was seeking a vote for being pro-Hindu and had even questioned the then chief election commissioner by calling him 'James Michael Lyngdoh' (a Christian name). Modi in other words has tried to give a message that it is not he who is under attack rather the entire Gujarati *'kaum'* (community) is besieged. As a Bengali, I can vouch that in the past for many years, the Left parties too had played the same card of 'Delhi hating Bengalis'. To substantiate this, the oft-repeated instance used to be that Congress leadership of Mahatma Gandhi and Jawaharlal Nehru had ignored and done injustice to Subhas Chandra Bose. And, Mamata Banerjee only seems to endorse this as she has taken up a new found cudgel on behalf of all regional parties and state governments for a stronger and meaningful federal structure of Indian polity.

In 2007, Modi had gone a step further. He took on Sonia Gandhi, the new reigning queen in Delhi as the UPA Government was already installed. "Do I, a son of Gujarat, look like a '*maut ka saudagar*' (merchant of death) you must pay Soniaben back for this insult to Gujarat".

Therefore, to suggest a more pragmatic and acceptable methodology to revive the faith of Muslims in Modi and importantly in Gujarat's administration, it is easier said than done. Yet, one can say, the response should be based on local and even 'kasba (hamlet)' wise approach instead of stereo-type models of the secular brigade or the minority appeasement of the most political class.

In dealing with social security issue, another vital point that needs to be understood especially in the context of a state like Gujarat is that some measures and policy framework - good as well as bad - would come even without being directed by the political will. The market force is by itself one catalyst for change. In Gujarat too, certain bold and far-reaching decisions like in land bank policy has come due to prevailing socio-political changes in other parts of the country. The Singur episode served as a telling picture of how land issue should not be mishandled. Ultimately, that had proved fatal for the Left Front in Bengal. Over the last few years, in developmental sphere Gujarat too in a neo-emerging generation of tech-savvy individuals have played a part. The IT savvy of the majority of people in urban pockets had encouraged unprecedented dependency on technology and thus enhanced the level of transparency in the government, said a senior state government official.

However, in the end it needs to be stated that typical to any dynamic society, Modi also faces an obvious challenge.

The burden of his past and the unfinished tasks in improving his image drags down his good works in the developmental sphere. I am saying this, despite the fact that the Modi camp including his senior party colleague, LK Advani, is asserting time and again that he is the most vilified Indian politician in the recent times and does not need any image makeover.

The greatest lesson that needs to be drawn from Modi phenomenon is that too much concentration of power on one-man or one set of people - chosen by that man - augurs dangerous for any democratic set up. What's wrong with Modi, is the same point that was wrong with Indira Gandhi running the Congress party and the government during her time. Even the ardent fan of Indira Gandhi and Congress loyalist would have to agree that she ruined governance by insisting upon a 'committed bureaucracy' and by destroying all democratic institutions. As a result, there is no gainsaying to point out that corruption was brought in all institutions in the country. Concentration of power in one hand would be a challenge in near future not only in BJP but in Indian polity itself.

The Election Commission's mandatory rule that internal democracy should be held in all parties had ended up as a farce with all political parties --- barring perhaps the Left parties. But with the Communists too, the senior category commands more than anything else.

Indian political parties largely san internal democracy. The Congress is truly the fountainhead of the current political culture in the country. The Congress is deep-soaked in its family sycophancy. Incidentally, the socialists variety has splintered into so many groups that one has lost the count. But each of these parties is essentially one-family control. Samajwadi is Mulayam Singh Yadav show, similarly RJD is Lalu Yadav's fiefdom, BSP has been a Mayawati's pocket-burrow, AIADMK, DMK, Trinamool Congress none offer any different criterion. Obviously, in Samajwadi Party, the mantle has gone to Junior Yadav, Akhilesh.

BJP leaders would insist on their claim for the once loved title of 'party with a difference'. But the saffron party is being remote controlled from Sangh Parivar fountainhead RSS, is no secret now. This became only obvious when RSS general secretary Mohan Bhagwat imposed his personal nominee from Maharashtra - a typical mofusil leader - Nitin Gadkari as the party president.

The assembly elections in early 2012 heralded a new paradigm shift in North India's politics which for long rested on caste, religion and goondaism. The UP mandate decisively in favour of Samajwadi Party perhaps proved a point that for the Junior Yadav, Akhilesh, the best trump card, and not without good reason, has been humility and ear-on-ground approach.

To many the battle in country's most populous state was ultimately between Akhilesh Yadav and Rahul Gandhi though it was BSP supremo Mayawati, who was handed over a convincing defeat.

Writing for my paper, *The Statesman*, on March 6, 2012, the day results were out, I wrote: "If a comparison is made between a limited overs cricket tournament and the just concluded assembly polls, undoubtedly Akhilesh Yadav, the youth icon of Samajwadi Party, is the man of the series".

The UP results wherein his party stormed back to power by increasing its vote share to near thirty per cent shows that his brand of politics had paid dividends. In 2009, post-Lok Sabha polls wherein Congress picked up good number of seats, his father had chosen him as the UP unit president. It was a daunting challenge. "We have to fight BSP and the Congress - the two parties in power and as well as stop BJP", he had said then and about three years since then he has exactly done that. Refusing to be dubbed as a simple beneficiary of dynastic hierarchy - as his father's son - Akhilesh, who had done Masters in Environmental Engineering from Sydney University, had brought in a new rhetoric and rhythm in socialistic politics.

Now, in the context of lesson from the mandate 2012 especially for the Modi camp and the BJP would be to realize that Samajwadi Party's victory has again revived the talk of fledgling Third Front. There is a further twist in the so-called non-Congress, non-BJP combination this time.

A key NDA constituent JD (U) of Nitish Kumar is giving mixed signals. During her trip to Delhi with the mission to replace Dinesh Trivedi as the railway minister by her protégé Mukul Roy; Mamata Banerjee already spoke about Federal Front. So, in the eventuality Nitish Kumar joins other regional satraps like Naveen Patnaik and Banerjee, BJP's dream of returning to power will simply fall. Of course, the BJP would definitely draw a satisfaction in the ouster of BSP in 2012 but that would deny Narendra Modi the chance to take a shot in 2014. But as it seen often, ultimately in politics, the real game boils down to the number game. If BJP has numbers, Modi will be in the reckoning.

Importantly, more so, if he can bring in votes and ultimately seats in the lower house of Indian Parliament. Otherwise, the country can have a Third Front government with the likes of Mulayam Singh Yadav as a strong contender. Moreover, Orissa's popular Chief Minister Naveen Patnaik, could be in reckoning this time. Till his time comes, Modi will be left almost licking his wounds trying to resurrect himself as a '*Vikas Purush* (development man)' and his admirers will be left contended to believe that he is the best Prime Minister, India is still to believe.

Axiom about LK Advani and others

As I reach the last part of the work on this, revision of the edited draft and postscript writing and essential one, I am reminded of the danger or risk that for every performing politician and more so in a vibrant democracy like ours, there are those whose motives are self-serving and malicious.

Now, this is no way to attempt to put either, Narendra Modi, Advani or Nitin Gadkari in one category or the other. The posterity will judge that best, maybe.

But it ought to be stated that Narendra Modi's or for that matter BJP's accomplishments and methods to achieve electoral success in post Rajiv Gandhi era in Indian polity spark off few crucial questions of means and ends, as the Father of the Nation, Mahatma Gandhi had often spoken about. How does these means and ends relate in effect in parliamentary democracy guided ultimately by electoral success or failure? Is electoral success so vital and what would follow then?

These questions broadly refer to the other political class too. How do Lalu Prasad or Mayawati's segmented appeal and corruption justify their success or failure? How does Congress absolve itself from the charge of creating vote banks by glorifying Urdu and playing minority (read Muslim) appeasement card in UP in 2012? Did Congress get the ultimate message that Muslim in Uttar Pradesh outright rejected their carrot and gave back Rahul Gandhi's party, the stick (read humbling defeat) in the elections?

Firstly, while talking about Advani, one must say that the truism about politics is that often charishmatic leaders like Advani, (who contributed the most for BJP's success) do not possess the vital luck and the right rhythm and flexibility to get the chance to lead a government or the country. Despite his glorious past, history will be no kinder to Advani. Since 2004, his political journey has been a test case of flirting with failures and mistakes. And mostly, they were self-inflicted flaws. If he thought 'India Shining' was a mistake, he should have corrected it on time. In more ways than one, Advani himself knew that with aging Vajpayee around; the 2004 general elections were more crucial for him as he would have been natural choice to succeed Vajpayee. Advani was already the Deputy Prime Minister.

Late Pramod Mahajan started working against him. No party leader tried to defend his remark on Jinnah.

Advani must have been accustomed to be boss deciding and guiding the party's destiny as well as calling shots for individual careers. From Sushma Swaraj to Venkaiah

Naidu to Pramod Mahajan, and not forgetting Narendra Modi, all were his hand-picked leaders and beneficiaries of his benevolence.

But the claim to remain the natural and legitimate player that too in a commanding position, was torpedoed by the blunder of 2005 – Jinnah is secular hara-kiri. Similarly, his blog on May 31, 2012, the day his party had called for Bharat Bandh against petrol price hike was equally self-destructive.

In between too, he has committed few other mistakes like total mishandling of 'cash-for-vote' episode in 2008 trial of strength in Lok Sabha. In what was said to be Dr Singh's crucial test, Advani staked his part that too --- significantly – probably at the instance of operators like Suddhendra Kulkarni. So much was the quantum of mistake that he was even pulled by then Lok Sabha Speaker Somnath Chatterjee for allowing BJP MPs to bring in table cash in the Lok Sabha. Calling Prime Minister 'the weakest Prime Minister' also did not help his case either.

In the case of Nitin Gadkari, he did not have much to claim except RSS blessings. While Narendra Modi's motivations and objectives were never a 'mystery', I presume there are serious contradictions and difficult issues in evaluating Gadkari. Not so successful in state politics, one thing was clear from very beginning that he was RSS protégé and was willing to play second fiddle anytime. His actions often puzzled hardcore BJP supporters. During the peak of anti-corruption crusade, led by Anna Hazare and that seemingly had put the UPA regime on the dock, Gadkari chose to take in one tainted minister of Mayawati, Babu Singh Kushwaha just before UP elections. Thus, it was not without good reason Congress general secretary Digvijaya Singh mocked at Gadkari saying; the BJP president was more of a 'businessman'.

However, it ought to be said that his initial achievement after he took over in December 2009 was to bring a semblance of stability in the party and prevent the party from disintegrating into numerous factions. But the latent divisions in the party remained palpably all throughout.

For Modi, I have earlier in this book said that he defies being categorized. In fact, Modi has made over the years an art from out of class stereotypes.

He is lethal to his rivals with unique combination of Hindutva chauvinist and development model and remains by far most active neta of our times. In course of working on this book, I had circulated a few questions among different categories of people. One query was how they would try to describe Narendra Modi.

Obviously, the responses were interesting. His admirers saying that he is 'future Prime Minister' some said he was anti-Muslim and communal.

But a neo-classic response came from a distant niece of mine (15-year-old) from Assam, who said, Modi to her resembles "a benevolent dictator who needs to rule India with decisiveness and strong hands". Another response called him, 'honest and incorruptible – except the corruption of power'.

In fact, these responses help to analyze many contradictions I faced while trying to focus on Modi's personality. I knew for once that he has used electoral polity to wield power and has used his ruthlessness to eliminate all rivalries in Gujarat both within BJP and outside. He also discarded without a trace of remorse leaders like Keshubhai Patel and the Late Haren Pandya. But the answers to the question whether he is such crude and dictatorial or these are only expected by-product and unintended ones for remaining in power remain only in the womb of time.

But having said these, I now come to yet another key aspect of the responses from the interviewees and thus here present a FAQ --- the frequently asked questions – on Modi.

FAQ on Narendra Modi

Question: When and where was Modi born?

• He was born on 17th September, 1950 at Vadnagar, a small town in Mehsana district of North Gujarat.

Question: Who were his parents?

• His father was Damodardas Mulchand Modi and mother was Heeraben. He was the third of the six children born to his parents. He is from Ghanchi community which belongs to Other Backward Classes.

Question: Some highlight of his personal life?

• Modi holds Masters Degree in Political Science. He is also said to have married Jashodaben Chimanlal, now a school teacher in hamlet called Rajosana. Modi's detractors often make this an issue and say as a married man, how he could be a RSS 'pracharak'. Modi had his schooling in Vadnagar.

Question: How did he have early plunge into politics/student politics?

• According to Modi's personal website, www. narendramodi.in, during the Indo-Pak war in the sixties, as a young boy, he had volunteered to serve the soldiers in transit at railway stations. In 1967, he served the flood-affected people of Gujarat. Endowed with excellent organizational capability, he was elected as the student leader of Akhil Bhartiya Vidyarthi Parishad, the student wing backed by the Sangh Privar.

Question: What are the roles he played in RSS?

• Modi played several important roles on various occasions including the 1974, Navnirman anti-corruption agitation and during the 19-month (June 1975 to January 1977) long emergency.

Question: When did he join BJP?

• He entered mainstream politics in 1987 by joining the BJP. Within a year, he was elevated to the level of General Secretary of the Gujarat unit.

Question: In early years, how did he contribute towards BJP's growth in Gujarat?

- Between 1988 and 1995, Modi emerged as a master strategist for BJP. He displayed his skills in organisational ability when he discharged the role in organizing LK Advani's Somnath to Ayodhya Rath Yatra and a similar march from Kanyakumari to Kashmir for the then BJP president MM Joshi. The ascent of BJP in power in Centre is largely attributed to these yatras as also party's growth in other states.

Question: What other responsibilities were given to him in the party?

- In 1995, he was appointed the National Secretary of the party and given the charge of five major states in India – a rare distinction for a young leader.

- In 1998, he was promoted as the general secretary (Organization), a post he held until October 2001, when he was chosen to be the Chief Minister of Gujarat to replace Keshubhai Patel.

Question: Any other highlight of his work for BJP?

- During his stint at the national level, Narendra Modi was given the responsibility to oversee the affairs of several state level units, including the sensitive and crucial state of Jammu and Kashmir and the north-eastern states. He was also in-charge of Madhya Pradesh in 1998.

Question: When was Modi first sworn in as the Chief Minister?

- He was first sworn in as Chief Minister on October 7, 2001.

Question: What's Panchamrit Yojana?

- This was conceived by Modi as a five-pronged strategy for an integrated development of Gujarat. These included industrial growth with focus appropriately on social sectors. And it also envisaged rebuilding Bhuj after the killer quake of January 2001.

Question: Which assembly seat in Gujarat did Modi first won in 2001-2002?

• Rajkot-II assembly seat. Earlier the seat was held by controversial Revenue Minister Vajubhai Vala. Subsequently, for 2002 December polls, he shifted to Maninagar assembly seat in Ahmedabad.

Question: How many seats BJP won in 2002 December polls?

• In December 2002 general elections, first since the Godhra carnage and the riots, the Modi government was voted back to power with a massive majority of 127 seats in a house of 182. In 2007 also, Modi was handed over a convincing victory this time bagging 119 seats.

Question: What's Modi's contribution vis-à-vis Narmada dam?

• Fighting against all odds, he ensured that the Narmada dam reached 121.9 m height. He even observed a fast to counteract those obstructing the construction. As against total central spending of Rs 10,000 crore for the dam, in 2006 alone, Modi government reportedly spent Rs 13,000 crore for the project.

Question: What's Sujalam Sufalam?

• It's a scheme to create a grid of water resources in Gujarat and is considered an innovative step towards water conservation and its appropriate utilization.

Question: Name some projects Modi government launched?

• Krishi Mahotsav, Chiranjeevi Yojana, Matru Vandana, Beti Bachao Campaign (save the girl child), Jyotigram Yojana, and Karmayogi Abhiyan – all aiming at multi-dimensional development of Gujarat. A Planning Commission study, supported by World Bank, has said that Gujarat offers an example of international best practice in roads management.

Question: International laurels bagged by his government

• Under the able leadership of Modi, Gujarat has bagged several awards and accolades including UN

Sasakawa Award for disaster reduction, Commonwealth Association for Public Administration and Management (CAPAM) award for innovations in governance, UNESCO award, CSI award for e-Governance.

Question: What's Vibrant Gujarat?

- Vibrant Gujarat is business summit convened by Modi government wherein business leaders and diplomats from across the globe throng in. It is considered as the masterstroke of putting Gujarat on the global map. Several state governments, including Bihar and West Bengal have tried to replicate the same.

Thus spake Narendra Modi: Quotes

- Today when people talk about development, they talk about Gujarat. When they talk about Gujarat, they talk about development that is; these are two sides of the same coin.
- Secularism is a term interpreted in many different ways by different people. For me, it has always been something very simple - putting India First.
- Dreams are not seen when you sleep, dreams are those that don't let you sleep. - On Motivation
- There is no red-tapism in my state, only red carpet. - On Governance
- T+IT=IT Indian talent + Information technology = India Tomorrow - On e-governance

Witty Quote:

- Manmohan Singhji, you are walking around like a body-builder just because we called you a weak prime minister. When LK Advani called you weak, he was not commenting on your chest size, your blood group or your eyesight, he was questioning the prime minister as an institution. (In 2009 election campaign)

Fact Sheet:

Godhra Attack not under POTA

In 2005, under the UPA-I, the Justice Jain POTA Review Committee had maintained that the Godhra train inferno of February 27, 2002 "was certainly not as a part of conspiracy envisaged under the provisions of POTA". An Office Memorandum on July 4, 2005 from Jag Ram, deputy secretary to the Home Ministry, New Delhi said that "the POTA Repeal Act, 2004 *inter alia* provides in terms of its Section 2(3) that when the Review Committee constituted by the Central Government is of the opinion that there is no prima facie ground for proceeding against the accused in a particular case under POTA, that case shall be deemed to have been withdrawn even if it has been taken cognizance of by the court".

It said on May 16, 2005, the Justice Jain POTA Review Committee "after appreciating the evidence ..... The Committee is of the considered view that this incident (Godhra station attack) had taken place on the date, time and place as alleged by the prosecution but certainly not as a part of conspiracy. This Committee, therefore, is of the view that the accused persons may be tried under the provisions of IPC, Indian Railways Act, and Prevention of Damages of Public Property Act, Bombay Police Act but not under the provisions of Prevention of Terrorism Act, 2002".

The memorandum was also directed to the Prime Minister's Office referring to an earlier communication PMO ID No. 805/21/C/14/2005 – Pol (of 14 February, 2005)

From the pages of history:

Q: What did Modi say about Vajpayee-Musharraf failed Agra Summit?

Answer: "Journey for peace talks have just begun. Defensive and offensive are subjective terms. Atalji is not merely a politician, but also a statesman. He was very clear about what he was doing before extending an invitation to the Pakistan President. The very fact that Musharraf had gone back without signing any agreement clearly shows that Atalji was not on the defensive, but on the offensive".

Q: Which Chief Election Commissioner, Modi had criticized and how?

Answer: Modi had flayed the then CEC JM Lyngdoh for delaying holding of assembly elections in Gujarat in 2002. He said at a rally, "For several months, the opposition has been after me to resign. When I did, they did not know what to do and started running to Delhi to seek Madam's help. They realised that James Michael Lyngdoh, the Election Commissioner of India, is their only saviour. Some journalists asked me recently, "Has James Michael Lyngdoh come from Italy?" I said I don't have his *janam patri*, I will have to ask Rajiv Gandhi...... James Michael Lyngdoh came and visited Ahmedabad and Vadodara. And then he gave a *fatwa* ordering that the elections can't be held". (Courtesy, *The Indian Express*)

Q: Which socialist leader had called Modi, 'a beacon of light'?

Answer: According to George Fernandes, Sarvodaya leader Jai Prakash Narayan had a fascination for youthful leadership of Narendra Modi in 1970s. "JP used to mention at least ten times a day that he was greatly fascinated by this youthful leader of Gujarat who has looked to him as 'Roshni (beacon of light)'," Fernandes had said during a peace yatra in Ahmedabad aftermath the riots in 2002.

Q: Who was Modi's security advisor in 2002 during and after the riots?

Answer: Former super cop KPS Gill.

Q: What did Modi tell in Ahmedabad in 2002 when Vajpayee had asked him to discharge 'Raj Dharma'?

Answer: "Sir, *wohi toh kar raha hoon* (Sir, I am doing that only)".

Q: Which 'Baba' did he compare UPA government with?

Answer: In May 2012, at a Mumbai rally, Modi compared UPA government with the darbar of controversial Nirmal Baba.

Q: What did anti-corruption crusader Anna Hazare tell about Modi government?

Answer: "The work done by Chief Ministers of Bihar (Nitish Kumar), and Gujarat (Narendra Modi) should be done by chief ministers of all states. I am not in support of any party, but the work they (Modi and Nitish Kumar) have done at the grassroots level is needed. (Anna had said on 11 April, 2011)

Q: What did Prime Minister Manmohan Singh say when Modi was denied visa in 2005?

Answer: The Prime Minister Manmohan Singh had described the US denial of visa to Modi, as "uncalled for" and said, "We respect the sovereign right to grant or refuse visa to any person. We do not believe that it is appropriate to use allegations or anything less than due legal process to make a subjective judgment to question a Constitutional authority in India".

Index

Some of our learned Authors

General S Padmanabhan; General VP Malik; Air Chief Marshal Fali Homi Major; Admiral Vishnu Bhagwat; Admiral Nirmal Verma; Admiral Arun Prakash; Vice Admiral Vijay Shankar; Lt Gen Arjun Ray; Dr A Sivathanu Pillai DRDO; Parvez Dewan IAS; Dhirendra Singh IAS; Kalyan Ray IAS; Sangeeta Goel IAS; HN Das IAS; Dr Surender Ghonkrokta IAS; Falguni Rajkumar IAS; G Sundaram IAS; PS Bhatnagar IAS; N Vittal IAS; PK Agrawal IAS; Sudhir S Baloeria IAS; NS Sisodia IAS; Dhirendra Singh IAS; Dr Yogendra Narain IPS; JK Bagchi IAS; TSR Subramanian IAS; Prakash Singh IPS; DC Nath IPS; Ajit Doval IPS; SP Mathur IPS; MK Dhar IPS; SK Datta IPS; HS Swan IPS; BR Lall IPS; PC Dogra IPS; DC Pathak IPS; ML Kumawat IPS; Dr. S Subramanian IPS; RK Ohri IPS; RB Sreekumar IPS; Kalyan K Mitra IPS; RS Gupta IPS; K Koshy IPS; Kuldeep Khoda IPS; Ajay Kashyap IPS; Dr N Dilip Kumar IPS; Dr Nazrul Islam IPS; Dr DV Guruprasad IPS; AP Maheshwari IPS; Loknath Behera IPS; Dr NC Asthana IPS; PM Nair IPS; Dr Sundari Nanda IPS; Keshav Kumar IPS; Dr Prateep V Philip IPS; Muktesh Chander IPS; Dr PS Pasricha IPS; VK Agarwal IRS; Virendra Gupta IFS; Lt Gen SK Sinha; Lt Gen Raj Kadyan; Lt Gen Mukesh Sabharwal; Lt Gen HB Kala; Lt Gen PC Katoch; Lt Gen Gautam Banerjee; Lt Gen Ashok Kapur; Vice Admiral Suresh Bangara; Lt Gen CK Kapur; Lt Gen NS Narahari; Lt Gen Chandra Shekhar; Lt Gen ML Chibber; Lt Gen Ashok Joshi; Lt Gen DB Shekatkar; Lt Gen SRR Aiyengar; Lt Gen Utpal Bhattacharyya; Lt Gen Kamal Davar; Lt Gen Amitav Mukherji; Maj Gen Nilendra Kumar; Maj Gen Vinod Saighal; Maj Gen VK Singh; Maj Gen Anjan Mukherjee; Maj Gen Raj Mehta; Maj Gen Samay Ram; Maj Gen Y Behl; Maj Gen GD Bakshi; Gen Deepak Kapoor; Air Marshal SR Deshpande; Air Marshal RC Bajpai; Air Chief Marshal PV Naik; Air Vice Marshal AK Tiwary; Air Cmde (Dr) CN Ghosh; Ambassador Kishan S Rana IFS; Cmde Ranjit B Rai; Capt (IN) Alok Bansal; VK Singal IRS; Sudha Raman; Brig Yash Mohan; Brig Trigunesh Mukherjee; Brig. MS Patial; Col PK Gautam; Col Arun Jha; Col MS Jaswal; Col Anil Shorey; Lt Col Anil Bhatt; Dr Harsh Vardhan; Ratan Sharda, Sudhakar Raje; Dr RK Tiwari; Anuj Dhar, Journalist; Ranjit Kumar, Journalist; SK Vikram; Gopal Chowdhuri; Dr Pramod Sharma; Swati Sharma, etc.